D1316808

THE
ROLLER
COASTER
LOVER'S COMPANION

THE
ROLLER COASTER
LOVER'S COMPANION

A Thrill Seeker's Guide to the World's Best Coasters

STEVEN J. URBANOWICZ

A CITADEL PRESS BOOK
Published by Carol Publishing Group

791.068
URB

Copyright © 1997 Steven J. Urbanowicz
All rights reserved. No part of this book may be reproduced in any form, except
by a newspaper or magazine reviewer who wishes to quote brief passages in
connection with a review.

A Citadel Press Book
Published by Carol Publishing Group
Citadel Press is a registered trademark of Carol Communications, Inc.

Editorial, sales and distribution, and rights and permissions inquiries should be addressed
to Carol Publishing Group, 120 Enterprise Avenue, Secaucus, N.J. 07094.

In Canada: Canadian Manda Group, One Atlantic Avenue, Suite 105, Toronto, Ontario
M6K 3E7

Carol Publishing Group books may be purchased in bulk at special discounts for sales
promotion, fund-raising, or educational purposes. Special editions can be created to
specifications. For details, contact Special Sales Department, Carol Publishing Group,
120 Enterprise Avenue, Secaucus, N.J. 07094.

Manufactured in the United States of America
10 9 8 7 6 5 4 3 2 1

Library of Congress Cataloging-in-Publication Data

Urbanowicz, Steven J.
    The roller coaster lover's companion : a thrill-seeker's guide to the world's best
coasters / Steven J. Urbanowicz.
        p.   cm.
    Includes index.
    ISBN 0-8065-1924-X (pb)
    1. Roller coasters.   I. Title.
GV1860.R64U83   1997
791'.06'8—dc21   97–25234
                                                                       CIP

Facing title page: Loch Ness Monster, Busch Gardens, Williamsburg.
(Courtesy of Busch Gardens)

Title page: Cedar Point's Magnum XL 200 (Courtesy of Dan Feicht, Cedar Point)

For my mother, Carolyn

The Great American Revolution at Six Flags Magic Mountain.

_14²⁵_

Contents

The author (left) enjoys the Phoenix at Knoebel's Amusement Resort with friends and coaster riding partners (left to right) Colleen Whyte, Robert Camuto, and Dennis McNulty. (Author's Collection)

Acknowledgments

I must thank all those in my life responsible for nurturing my love of amusement parks and roller coasters.

First and foremost, my mom, Carolyn, who never stopped taking me to amusement parks when I was a child, just because she knew I loved them. Her stories of riding the Rye, New York, Airplane at Playland (and her vow never to ride another roller coaster ever again) sparked in me an interest in these rides that has never vanished.

Thanks also to my grandmother, Jean, a true thrill seeker, who loved all the rides at the park and took me on them with her. To my aunt Doris Titus and her friend Ann Tomza, my riding partners on my first big roller coaster, the Cyclone, at my beloved Palisades Amusement Park. To Doris's daughter, Brook Baxter, my cousin, who I took to parks when she was just a child and I was passing out of my teens, a time when I foolishly began to think that parks were for children. Thanks, Brook, for keeping me going long enough so that I had time to come to my senses.

Thanks to my coaster-riding buddies, especially Bobby Nagy, Robert Camuto, Dennis and DeAnn McNulty, Colleen Whyte, Robert and Joan Api, Sam Marks, Keith Johnson, Sonia Stanford, Bret Malone, Joe Radomile, Bill Galvin, Glenn Pyewell, and Ed McInerney. Let the good times roll! In memory of Richard Klimek and Michael Bent.

Thanks and gratitude to Janice Lifke at Cedar Point and to Joanna Puglisi and Mike Barley at Dorney Park for all their help and, most important, their friendship.

Thanks to Zhi Zhi Loya at Six Flags Great Adventure for a most fateful telephone call. Also to the park's Skull Mountain, for putting me in the right place at the right time.

And to all the parks, manufacturers, and individuals who supplied information or photographs, I am forever in your debt.

Wild Thing, Valleyfair! (Courtesy of Dan Feicht)

Introduction

Why do we ride roller coasters? Why would people allow themselves to be lifted to impossible heights, only to plummet crazily to the ground? Who would want to careen through insane curves with their bodies bouncing around like rowboats in the Atlantic during a hurricane?

There may never be a satisfactory answer. For each and every one of us, the reason we venture aboard these monstrous thrill machines is different. Some of us are looking for death-defying kicks. Others may simply be looking for a good scream. And, believe it or not, there are those who think roller coasters are just plain, honest-to-goodness fun!

Whatever the reason for coaster riding, it is obvious that the number of folks who do participate in this passive "sport" is high. Over 200 million people visit amusement and theme parks each year, in the United States alone. At each and every park, the most-ridden attraction is always a roller coaster. At parks with multiple coasters, it is not unusual to find that all the most popular rides are coasters.

The parks know that coasters are what the guests come to ride, and it is not out of the question for a new coaster to be added every season or two. A brand-new wood or steel scream machine can cost anywhere from $2 million to $13 million, but it can also increase the park's attendance dramatically, sometimes as much as 30 percent. A worthwhile return on the investment.

A major thrill ride may take as long as a year to be installed. Construction and landscaping alone can add $2 to $3 million to the total cost, but the parks are more than willing to make these huge investments, as they only have to look at their profits to see the obvious: if they build it, we will come. Again and again.

For those of us who love these magnificent creations, these are truly exciting times. A major "coaster war" has existed for years and shows no sign of letting up. The race is on to build the biggest, wickedest, must stunning coaster in the world. More than fifty new rides open each season. Most are

〰〰

Roller Coaster Fact: Leap-the-Gap, an early twentieth-century design, featured (surprise!) a gap in the track. Trains were supposed to jump across and land safely on the other side. It never opened to the public, because it was discovered in the experimental stages that the course of the vehicle would vary depending on the weight of the passengers it carried.

〰〰

good, some are exceptional, and a few are legendary from the moment the train crests the lift-hill.

A good roller coaster need not be the biggest, longest, or fastest. What is important, what does make a good ride, is "pacing": that is, how the hills, turns, and speed are placed in the finished package to create the total ride experience. It takes much more than an engineering degree to build a great coaster. An acute sense of drama and intimate knowledge of psychology must also be employed.

Contrary to an all-too-common belief, roller coasters are extremely safe devices. Of course, sometimes there are mechanical problems, but they occur so rarely that one need not even be concerned about them. Serious accidents do happen on occasion, but these are almost always due to the foolish behavior of passengers. It would seem that for some, the thrill of riding a coaster is insufficient, so they attempt to enhance the experience by standing up, or switching seats, or any number of asinine antics. That DO NOT STAND UP sign is there for a reason, folks. Because rules are sometimes ignored, parks have invented ways to protect riders from themselves; most coaster trains now have at least four different types of restraints. Some of these may take a little of the edge off the ride experience, but let's face it—that's an easy compromise to make to ensure that everyone makes it back to the station safe and sound, even the idiotic ones. In some states, rider misbehavior is considered a misdemeanor crime.

Regarding other safety concerns: No, coasters cannot jump the tracks; they are locked into place. No one has ever been thrown from a coaster because the ride itself was too rambunctious. Lap-bars do not fly open during the ride. Trains have never fallen apart while in motion. Even the oldest coaster has never collapsed with a train full of riders going through the course. There are too many myths to count. Just keep in mind that statistics show that walking through doorways has caused more injuries than coasters. At the parks, so too have carousels.

Roller Coaster Fact: Among the more famous admirers of roller coasters are Matt Dillon, Michael Jackson, Natalie Cole, Kristy McNichol, and the late Vincent Price, Judy Garland, and Elvis Presley.

So feel free to ride a roller coaster, with gleeful abandon. And while we'll probably never know why we do, we must like whatever it is that these monuments of kinetic sculpture provide to us. Whether it be physical, emotional, or psychological gratification (or perhaps spiritual or intellectual), between March and November, it is our season. Our time to give in to the irresistible urge to ride a roller coaster.

It is our time to take the plunge into the abyss, fully aware that we'll want to take that plunge again.

Before We Begin Our Ride: How to Use This Book

The Roller Coaster Lover's Companion is designed to tell you everything you need to know to get the most out of roller coaster riding.

Chapter 1 provides a brief history of coasters, detailing the types of rides that have existed since the first person rolled down a track, to the present day mega-monsters. Chapter 2 tells you about the builders of the different types of coasters you're likely to encounter in your travels.

In chapter 3, you'll discover many of the little secrets coaster enthusiasts have been privy to for years, so you can enjoy coastering more: from which seat is the best to money-saving tips on admission. Chapter 4 describes all types of coasters and coaster technology to enable the novice to better understand what he or she is getting into. (There's also a glossary at the end of the book.) In chapters 5 and 6, you'll find top ten lists of the best wood and steel roller coasters, respectively. The top ten must-visit parks with the most extensive coaster collections are listed in chapter 7.

Chapter 8 lists the important roller coasters on each continent (listed by country, then state or province, then park) and includes *The Roller Coaster Lover's Companion*'s exclusive rating system, created to help you determine if a certain ride is too wild, too mild, or just right for you. Chapter 9 recommends what parks to combine to make truly stupendous mini-vacations, all designed around coastering.

As you ride more and more coasters, use the lists provided in chapters 10 and 11 to check off the coasters you have conquered, which are now on your "track record." Also, use these lists as an easy locator guide, to pinpoint exactly where each and every ride that interests you resides. And finally, check out the top five lists in chapter 12, comparing them to the list of favorites that you yourself might have already been creating.

Now get ready to roll!!!

THE
ROLLER
COASTER
LOVER'S COMPANION

1 FROM RUSSIA, WITH LOVE

The first roller coaster, in the form that we know today, was built in New York's own Coney Island in 1884. It was a scant fifteen feet tall, and ran at a whopping top speed of four miles per hour.

We've come a long way, baby!

Today's roller coasters top out at well over two hundred feet, and speeds of almost 90 mph are not uncommon. Some are made of wood, more are made of steel. Modern coasters also go upside down (currently, eight inversions are the maximum). Passengers enjoy these contraptions sitting, standing, or hanging with their legs dangling below them. In short, coasters don't just go up and down any more.

While usually considered a purely American form of entertainment, these rides have their ancestry in a much more intriguing place than Brooklyn, New York, and it wasn't some carnival barker who thought them a viable diversion.

You see, the first folks to board a vehicle and roll down sloping hills for sport were guests at the Russian Imperial Summer Palace during the late eighteenth century. The person who devised this avant-garde pleasure was the palace's occupant, Catherine the Great, and even she had to get the idea from somewhere.

It was during the sixteenth century that the first ice slides were built. These were wooden structures with steep ramps thickly coated with ice, and passengers took turns sliding down aboard sleds fitted with runners. A popular pastime for over two hundred years, the ice slides had only one

Opposite page: Thunder Hawk, Dorney Park, one of the world's oldest operating roller coasters. (Courtesy of Dorney Park)

problem—they could only operate during the cold of the winter season. Catherine the Great wanted to slide during the summer season as well, so she had her sleds fitted with wheels. The world has been coasting ever since.

The term "roller coaster" would find its origins in a French adaptation of the Russian ice slides. The climate in Paris proved to be unsuitable for ice slides, so ramps were fitted with rollers upon which standard sleds with runners would coast—hence, "roller coaster." This arrangement was soon abandoned in favor of grooved wooden ramps and sleds with wheels, but the name roller coaster remains in use to this day.

The rides were so popular that they inspired innovations to improve each new one built. The first rides built in both Russia and France required their passengers to climb to the top of a tower in order to embark on their thrilling journey, which consisted of a simple single in-line drop. In the early nineteenth century, the people of France built the Belleville Mountains and the Promenades Aériennes. Both rides featured cars securely locked to the track, guide rails to keep them on course, much higher speeds, and greater thrills than ever before.

Meanwhile, some thrill riding was beginning to occur in the United States as well. In eastern Pennsylvania, an eighteen-mile-long incline railway, formerly used for transporting coal, was turned into a public attraction known as the Mauch Chunk Scenic Railway. Its railroad cars were hauled by steam engine to the top of the mountain, then simply coasted back down to the bottom. A brakeman was on duty at all times to see that the speed didn't get out of hand. Traces of the Mauch Chunk Scenic Railway still exist, and the area has since been declared a National Historic Landmark.

Slides similar to the Russian and French versions began appearing in the United States, but it wasn't until 1884 that a truly historic roller coaster event took place. The Switchback Railway opened for business on 10th Street in Coney Island, the world-famous Brooklyn, New York, beach resort. Located roughly where that famed Coney Island Cyclone resides today, the Switchback Railway is regarded as the first "modern" roller coaster ever built; that is, it featured an undulating track, with vehicles seeming to defy the law of gravity as they coasted over these hills. Legend has it that LaMarcus A. Thompson, the Switchback's inventor, was a Sunday school teacher and preacher, who created this milestone attraction to divert young men from frequenting the beer gardens that were popular at the time.

Whatever his reasons, the ride was enormously popular. It consisted of two side-by-side tracks, and passengers had to climb to the top of a platform to board the train. It was pushed out of the station and came to a stop at ground level some 600 feet down the beach. There, passengers would climb to the top of another tower (sometimes they had to help push the car up

A "coasting party" at Coney Island. (*Frank Leslie's Illustrated Newspaper,* July 24, 1886)

there, too), where the vehicle would be switched to the return track and pushed out for the return trip. An oval-track roller coaster debuted at Coney Island later that same year without these undesirable features.

In 1885, the first full-circuit roller coaster with a lift-cable was built. Philip Hinkle's Gravity Pleasure Road became the most popular attraction at Coney Island and started a wave of roller coaster construction across the country.

Not to be left out, LaMarcus Thompson began building coasters that included dark tunnels with painted scenery in them. His first, the Oriental

Scenic Railway, opened in Atlantic City, New Jersey, in 1886. At the time, he patented his attraction. Since that day, all roller coasters built in the United States have been referred to as "scenic railways" by the U.S. Patent Office.

By 1900, Coney Island had the first looping roller coaster. It was built entirely of wood and featured a single, completely round loop, which would viciously snap riders' heads, causing whiplash. The Flip-Flap, as it was known, attracted more viewers than riders, and its single two-passenger car did not allow the ride to make any money. The head snap was improved soon afterward on Loop-the-Loop, one of which opened in Coney Island, the other in Atlantic City. The shape of the loop was changed from the perfectly round circle to an ellipse, or teardrop-shaped (clothoid) loop. Passengers sailed through the inversion with nary a physical complaint. Unfortunately, single cars kept the capacity down on these rides as well, and they became financial failures. Looping roller coasters would not be built again until the 1970s; capacity problems were solved, and building material had changed from wood to steel, but the shape of the loop would be the same teardrop configuration used in the early part of the century.

Roller coasters were being built everywhere during the early 1900s. The usual design for the rides at the time was a figure eight, with gentle dips the main thrill. Cars would run freely on the multilevel track, with wooden guide rails keeping the vehicle on track. A prime example of this type of ride still exists at Lakemont Park in Altoona, Pennsylvania. A National Historic Landmark, it is the oldest roller coaster in the world. After being closed for many years, it is undergoing restoration for a reopening.

As the race to build the biggest, most thrilling roller coaster continued, it was soon discovered that existing methods of construction and safety features were dramatically insufficient. John Miller is generally regarded as the father of the modern roller coaster, because it was he who added to the cars wheels that ran under the track, keeping the trains in place during high-speed drops and turns. Miller also developed the locking lap-bars, anti-rollback ratchets, and other safety devices that are still in use on today's coasters. Without John Miller's inventions, we would not have the wild thrill rides of today. Miller designed rides featuring high humps, one after another, all with steep drops. A good example of a John Miller ride still operates at Geauga Lake, in Aurora, Ohio, a Cleveland suburb. Known as the Big Dipper, it is one of the oldest operating coasters in the country, and a prime example of the wildness that can be found in what is by today's standards a small roller coaster.

With the advent of Miller's inventions, any type of design could now be executed. Near-vertical drops, heart-stopping spirals, and vicious trick-track became the order of the day. The Roaring Twenties was the Golden Age for, among other things, roller coasters. Literally thousands were built, each attempting to outdo the last in size and thrills. Frank Prior and Fred Church

Raging Wolf Bobs is based on the Bobs at Riverview Park in Chicago, which closed in 1967. (Courtesy of Geauga Lake)

built Bobs coasters—spiraling, swooping scream machines. One of these, the Airplane at Playland in Rye, New York, is regarded as the greatest roller coaster ever built (sadly, it was torn down in 1957). In fact, of the many rides Prior and Church built, only two still operate, and only one is truly indicative of the typical Prior and Church design—the Giant Dipper at Belmont Park in San Diego, California.

Similar to Bobs designs were Harry Traver's Cyclone Safety Coasters. These rides also featured the spirals and swoops found in Prior and Church's Bobs coasters, but each was pitched much more severely, with some 85-degree banking not uncommon. Traver built only four Cyclone Safety Coasters. Three were removed rather quickly, but one, the Cyclone at Crystal Beach, Ontario, Canada, lasted twenty years (closing in 1946) and was known as the most frightening roller coaster ever built. Legend has it that a full-time nurse was on duty in the loading station at all times. The Cyclone and the Rye Playland Airplane are the two roller coasters that any serious fan of roller coasters would wish he or she could go back in time to experience.

Roller Coaster Fact: A man riding the late, great Bobs at Chicago's Riverview Park stood up and turned to wave at his family while his train was traveling up the ride's lift-hill. He was promptly knocked out of the coaster car by the ride's DO NOT STAND UP sign and fell to his death.

The severe nature of 1920s roller coasters can be experienced today to its fullest effect on the Cyclone at Coney Island, New York. Built in 1927, this National Historic Landmark, although not truly indicative of the swirling masterpieces built during its time period, features all the steep drops and tight roughhouse curves a roller coaster lover could want. It is the mother of all existing wooden roller coasters, and the one ride that all other coasters are measured against and aspire to be as good as.

Although coasters continued to be built, the Depression spelled the end to the widespread construction of the 1920s. During that time, many parks closed, and their roller coasters were torn down. With the onset of World War II, followed immediately by the advent of television, roller coasters rapidly began to disappear. Two thousand roller coasters worldwide dwindled down to two hundred. Amusement parks became shabby, shady operations, and poor maintenance led to safety hazards. No one cared about parks anymore; people had found other things to do with their leisure time.

But in July 1955, an event took place that would signal the rebirth of the amusement park: Walt Disney opened Disneyland, the nation's first "theme park." Six Flags followed in 1961, opening Six Flags Over Texas in the Dallas–Fort Worth metroplex. The arrival of the theme parks (of which forty to fifty were built in the ensuing twenty years) coincided with the final operating seasons of some of the nation's greatest amusement parks, including Chicago's Riverview and northern New Jersey's Palisades Amusement Park. But one thing was very clear. The parks that survived would likely prosper,

Roller Coaster Fact: Shortly after World War II, a man riding the Coney Island Cyclone began screaming. When it was over, he turned to his riding partner and said, "I feel sick." Not unusual—except that these were the first words he had uttered in years. Shell-shock suffered during the war had left him speechless until that moment.

Cyclone, Coney Island, New York. The 1927 original is still one of the most thrilling rides in the world. (Courtesy of Bobby Nagy)

and the new theme parks were a hit. Along with this renaissance in parks came a rebirth of the roller coaster.

This time, however, things were different. Disney and Six Flags built roller coasters using a new type of tubular steel track. Disney's Matterhorn, opened in 1959, featured a smoothness of ride and a deafening silence never before experienced on a coaster. When Six Flags debuted its Runaway Mine Train, there was incontestable proof that the roller coaster was back—but in an altered form. Coasters were now designed to attract families, and nothing in the ride was too severe or frightening, so no family member, from the youngest to the oldest, would hesitate to ride.

Soon that would change. At exactly the time that the Palisades Amusement Park Cyclone came crashing down, a new wooden roller coaster was under construction at a brand-new theme park outside of Cincinnati, Ohio. When Kings Island opened in 1972, so did the Racer, a dual-track masterpiece designed by

The Kings Island Racer heralded the return of the wooden roller coaster. (Courtesy of Paramount's Kings Island)

〜〜〜〜〜〜〜〜〜〜〜〜〜〜〜〜〜〜〜〜〜〜〜〜〜〜〜〜〜〜〜

Roller Coaster Fact: A bizarre fashion trend during the 1960s was the disposable paper dress. One woman found out just how disposable these frocks were when she wore one on a coaster. During the ride, the wind tore the dress off her, and she arrived back in the station stark naked.

〜〜〜〜〜〜〜〜〜〜〜〜〜〜〜〜〜〜〜〜〜〜〜〜〜〜〜〜〜〜〜

John Allen. The Racer is widely known as "the second coming," for it created a great deal of interest in the giant roller coaster again and spurred a building boom in large wooden roller coasters. Six Flags followed the next year with the Great American Scream Machine in its Georgia park, and the race was on once again to build the longest, tallest, fastest, and best roller coaster in the world. The title holders have changed almost every season since then.

But something else was happening in the world of roller coasters. Almost simultaneously, two California parks, Six Flags Magic Mountain and Knott's Berry Farm, opened steel looping coasters, the kind that have become the mainstay of today's parks. Knott's Roaring Twenties Corkscrew featured a double upside-down spiral, while Magic Mountain's Great American Revolution soared passengers through a single 360-degree loop. Ever since, all hell has been breaking loose!

For many reasons, theme parks have become places to take inexpensive mini-vacations, so they have remained extremely popular. Most of the older, smaller parks have also been doing quite well. The revenues generated have enabled park owners to invest what at times seem to be insane amounts of money on new thrill rides. Through all of this, the roller coaster has remained the most popular attraction at the parks, so in the time since the amusement park revival, we've seen more incredible forms of thrilling roller coasters built than that old Switchback inventor LaMarcus Thompson could have ever dreamed of.

The 1970s finished in a big way with the Beast at Paramount's Kings Island, which at 7,400 feet is still the world's longest wooden roller coaster. The single loop of Magic Mountain's Revolution has given way to the eight-inversion screamfest Dragon Khan at Port Aventura in Tarragona just outside of Barcelona, Spain. 1984 saw the world debut of the stand-up roller coaster, the King Cobra at Paramount's Kings Island, as well as the first successful suspended roller coasters, the Big Bad Wolf at Busch Gardens in Williamsburg, Virginia, and the XLR-8 at Six Flags Astroworld in Houston, Texas. The 1980s ended with the first coaster ever to break the 200-foot height barrier, the Magnum XL-200 at Sandusky, Ohio's Cedar Point. In 1992 Batman—The Ride came on line as the first inverted, outside-looping, chair-lift-style coaster.

〜〜〜〜〜〜〜〜〜〜〜〜〜〜〜〜〜〜〜〜〜〜〜〜〜〜〜〜〜〜〜〜〜〜

Roller Coaster Fact: The Lake Placid Bobsleds at Palisades Amusement Park in New Jersey was the world's tallest roller coaster at 125 feet. Only a few seasons after it was built, the Bobsleds ride was torn down. The Bobsleds, however, held the record for world's tallest coaster for nearly forty years. Until the debut of the Beast at Paramount's Kings Island in 1979, no coaster had been built that was taller than the Bobsleds 125-foot height.

〜〜〜〜〜〜〜〜〜〜〜〜〜〜〜〜〜〜〜〜〜〜〜〜〜〜〜〜〜〜〜〜〜〜

As we approach the millennium, linear induction motors are launching roller coasters to new heights, at speeds of 100 mph, doing away with the traditional lift-hill clattering of the past 110 years. Meanwhile, during all of these amazing technological advances, new wooden roller coasters like the Riverside Cyclone, Texas Giant, Hershey Wildcat, and Great White have been built in the grand style of the 1920s, and have been instant hits.

And to think, all of this, because someone wanted people to find something better to do with their time than drink beer!

2 THRILL MACHINES, THRILL MAKERS

Every roller coaster ever built works on a very basic scientific principle: what goes up must come down.

It is this simple law that is used to design all roller coasters. The force of gravity dictates the height of every hill after the initial lift-hill, and inertia determines how long the track length can be, depending on the height first attained by the structure.

In the days before computers and ultra-scientific equations, roller coaster builders designed their rides in a rather seat-of-the-pants manner. They would build their ride, and if the train of cars did not make it through the complete circuit, they would adjust hill heights accordingly.

This relatively unscientific approach sometimes resulted in rides with exceptionally high g-forces. Small "rabbit hop" hills positioned immediately after larger deep dips would occasionally produce severe "negative g's," lifting passengers up out of the seat. These moments, which roller coaster lovers refer to as "airtime," occur because the heavier train is being rapidly pulled down a hill while the much lighter passenger is still being projected in an upward motion. While today's computer-designed coasters still frequently provide these thrilling weightless moments, they are much less severe and much more controlled. For a good example of negative g's at their unbridled best, try the Comet at the Great Escape Fun Park in Lake George, New York. Originally built in 1946 at Crystal Beach Park in Ontario, Canada, this masterpiece was constructed in the days before computers dictated how much a roller coaster could throw the passenger around in the car. The Comet was relocated to the Great Escape in 1994, with no changes made to its design, and it features airtime on each and every hill.

The Comet also contains many moments of lateral gravity. Old-time roller coasters quite commonly featured turns that were designed flat and

~~~~~~

Roller Coaster Fact: The Coney Island Cyclone has inspired no fewer than five copies currently operating worldwide: Texas Cyclone at Six Flags Astroworld; Georgia Cyclone, Six Flags Over Georgia; Psyclone, Six Flags Magic Mountain (California); Viper, Six Flags Great America (Illinois); and White Canyon, Yomiuriland, Tokyo, Japan.

~~~~~~

were taken at high speeds, slamming passengers sideways to the outside of the turn. On some rides, this would cause passengers to collide with each other or, at the very least, careen into the side of the roller coaster car. On the more severe rides, broken ribs would not be surprising. The Great Escape Comet features several of these lateral slamming moments; fortunately, none of them are of the rib-breaking variety.

Today, computers determine the degree to which negative and lateral gravity will affect the passenger. If the results in a computer model are too severe, the coaster designer can lower the hill or bank the track more gently. Coaster trains are also now equipped with lap-bars that prevent the passenger from lifting out of the seat too precariously, and most rides now have seat dividers to keep side-to-side movement at a minimum.

No matter how computer-controlled these devices get, in the long run they still work the same way the roller coasters of yesteryear did. On a recent excursion of mine to an amusement park, weather conditions and an insufficient number of passengers to weight the train properly caused one roller coaster train to stop dead at the top of a hill, stranding passengers in a driving rain a hundred feet in the air. While this was a modern ride, built with all the new-fangled computer technology we now possess, the solution to the problem was quite primitive: maintenance workers had to climb the structure, attach a cable to the train, and winch the train over the hill so that it could continue along the circuit. That is, in the end, the beauty of roller coasters. No matter what magical gadgetry is attached to them, they inevitably operate in the same way they have for over one hundred years. Gravity still rules the day; track and wheels, in basically the same configuration as on 1910 coasters, are still standard; a simple link-chain still gets the train to the top of the highest hill; and the screams of the passengers haven't even come close to changing since the first passenger boarded the Switchback Railway in 1884.

THE BUILDERS

It's hard to believe that such primitive devices could cost $12 million or more, or that so many very successful companies would be in the business of building them. But that's the cost for a modern scream machine, and builders of today have attained an almost celebrity status. For roller coaster enthusiasts, the famous designers of the past are saints.

Philadelphia Toboggan Coasters

The Philadelphia Toboggan Company, opened in 1904, has built some of the best wooden roller coasters in the world. The father of the modern roller coaster, John Miller, designed some of his earliest works for the company. Miller's protégé Herbert Schmeck followed in the master's footsteps, with sharply pitched hill designs producing negative g's similar to those of Miller's coasters. Schmeck designs still in operation include the Yankee Cannonball at Canobie Lake Park in Salem, New Hampshire, and the Phoenix at Knoebel's Amusement Resort, Elysburg, Pennsylvania (the Phoenix was originally known as the Rocket, operating in Playland, San Antonio, Texas, until its relocation to Pennsylvania in 1985).

John Allen became PTC's chief designer during the 1950s, and he is the man most responsible for the roller coaster renaissance of the 1970s. His Racer at Paramount's Kings Island (1972), Great American Scream Machine at Six Flags Over Georgia (1973), and Screamin' Eagle at Six Flags St. Louis (1976) were each responsible for a new wave of roller coaster fever.

PTC—now known as Philadelphia Toboggan Coasters, and under the direction of Tom Rebbie and Bill Dauphinee—continues to be a major force in the roller coaster business. While the company no longer designs or builds coasters, it is responsible for the manufacturing of roller coaster trains, station air gates, and other vital equipment. Today, trains made by PTC are in operation on almost every wooden roller coaster in the world.

The John Miller Company

John Miller (formerly of PTC) founded Miller and Baker with Harry Baker in 1920. In 1923, the pair split, and Miller formed his own company. Rides from his company still operating include all three wooden roller coasters at Kennywood in West Mifflin, Pennsylvania. Miller later partnered with Norman Bartlett to create the Flying Turns, a trackless roller coaster whose trains ran freely within a carved-out wooden trough. Several of these rides were built in the 1930s, the largest of which, the Lake Placid Bobsleds at New Jersey's Palisades Amusement Park, was considered the most frightening. Its 125-foot lift-hill gave it the distinction of being the first roller coaster to be over 100 feet in height. Although the ride closed in 1946, another roller coaster approaching that height would not be built until 1979: Kings Island's Beast. No Flying Turns rides still exist, but modern incarnations of this type of ride can be found at several parks, most notably Paramount's Kings Dominion in Virginia. The park's Avalanche, although built of steel, closely reproduces the experience of the older ride.

Harry Baker's company, meanwhile, is responsible for the building of the world-famous Cyclone at Coney Island. Today, the Cyclone is still in operation and is one of the best roller coasters in the world.

Harry Traver
Prior and Church

Both Harry Traver's Cyclone Safety Coasters and Prior and Church's Bobs design, discussed in chapter 1, were renowned for the "spiral dip": that is, a turn during which a drop is executed. While none of Traver's frighteningly severe rides still exist, two Prior and Church coasters do. The Giant Dipper at Belmont Park in San Diego, California, is indicative of the spiraling nature of these designers' signature creations, while the other, the Dragon Coaster at Playland in Rye, New York, is not. Dragon, although an extremely long ride, was built as a milder alternative to the pair's infamous Airplane, considered by many to be the greatest roller coaster ever built. Its flat turns and shallow drops still offer thrills, but not the kind that Prior and Church normally provided.

Arrow Dynamics

The first steel roller coaster to achieve star status was Disneyland's Matterhorn. Built in 1959, it was the first to use a tubular steel track, and Arrow was the company responsible. Arrow went on to develop the family-style mine train coasters that became prevalent at the theme parks during the 1960s. The company is also renowned for introducing a ride that has become a staple at nearly every park in the world: the log flume.

Arrow really took the amusement industry by storm by being the first to reintroduce the concept of looping steel roller coasters to a world ready for a new way to be thrilled. The company's Roaring Twenties Corkscrew debuted in 1974 at Knott's Berry Farm in California. It topped out at a height of 70 feet, and during the course, riders were flipped upside down during a double spiral. The coaster currently operates as the Gravity Defying Corkscrew at Silverwood Theme Park in Athol, Idaho.

Paramount's Kings Island Vortex, installed in 1987, is a good example of how truly twisted Arrow Dynamics's looping coasters became. (Courtesy of Bobby Nagy)

After this historic debut, Arrow continued to build larger, more dramatic variations, soon incorporating 360-degree loops, double-flipping boomerangs, and direction-changing sidewinders. Although the company's looping steel roller coasters would eventually approach 200 feet in height, they still incorporated the same inversion elements made popular during the 1970s. Among Arrow's most thrilling looping coasters are the Loch Ness Monster at Busch Gardens in Williamsburg, Virginia, the Vortex at Paramount's Kings Island in Cincinnati, Ohio, and the Steel Phantom at Kennywood in West Mifflin, Pennsylvania, a giant monster that incorporates a 225-foot-long drop down a hillside and features speeds over 80 mph.

Arrow introduced the suspended roller coaster in 1984. Trains on this type of coaster hang below the track and swing wildly with every turn. Among the best are the Big Bad Wolf at Busch Gardens in Williamsburg, Virginia, the Ninja at Six Flags Magic Mountain in Valencia, California, and Top Gun, a movie-themed extravaganza in Cincinnati's Paramount's Kings Island.

The company ended the 1980s in a big way. Cedar Point in Ohio had asked the company to build a large, traditional-profile roller coaster out of steel: traditional in that it would feature no loops, corkscrews, etc., but the more familiar deep drops, camel backs, and rabbit hops that had character-ized smaller wooden roller coasters for a century. While it started out as a 180-foot-tall project, it soon grew to 205 feet, becoming the first roller coaster in the world ever to break the 200-foot barrier. The appropriately named Magnum XL-200 is still the park's most famous ride, and its tranquil setting along the shores of Lake Erie belies its rambunctious nature.

Arrow went on to build other non-looping steel giants, among them the Pepsi Max Big One at Blackpool Pleasure Beach in England and Desperado, a 209-foot-tall behemoth that operates as an alternative attraction at Buffalo Bill's Resort and Casino in Stateline, Nevada.

Arrow Dynamics has several interesting projects currently in the plan-ning stages. One of them, the Pipeline, is a novel idea featuring trains that ride between the tubular steel tracks rather than on top of or below them, enabling the trains to negotiate in-line heartline spirals (a forward-moving in-line inversion, which turns in a barrel-roll motion, so the rider's center of gravity shifts to the heart).

Togo

The Togo Company of Japan has been in the amusement business longer than Arrow, building all types of amusement rides in its native country. In the United States, the company caused a sensation in 1984 with the debut of the world's first looping steel coaster to have its passengers ride standing up: the King Cobra at Paramount's Kings Island (Ohio). Similar rides soon appeared at Paramount's Kings Dominion (Virginia) and Paramount Canada's Wonderland (Ontario).

The company next introduced the Ultra Twister at Six Flags Great Adventure in New Jersey, in which six-passenger vehicles were pulled up a 90-degree lift-hill to a height of 97 feet, only to plunge down an 85-degree drop (still one of the world's steepest roller coaster drops), then execute heartline spirals, both forward and in reverse (on a transfer track). Ultra Twister now operates at Six Flags Astroworld in Houston, Texas, modified with a still-steep 45-degree lift-hill, but retaining the steep first drop and multidirection heartline spins.

In 1988, the company built the Bandit, a huge non-looping terrain steelie. With a lift height of 167 feet and a vertical spread of 256 feet, it became the world's tallest coaster and perhaps served as inspiration to Arrow and Cedar Point for the following year's Magnum XL-200.

1995 saw the debut of the mega-coaster, a standard steel roller coaster capable of negotiating in-line spirals. The world's first installation went on line at Six Flags Great Adventure and is known as the Viper. A much larger

Great Adventure's Viper, and an example of a heartline spiral. (Courtesy of Six Flags Great Adventure)

variation opened at New York New York Hotel and Casino in Las Vegas. The Manhattan Express is 203 feet tall and features a standard loop as well as a heartline flip; its cars are designed to look like little yellow taxis.

Togo is the builder of the coaster that currently holds the record for tallest in the world. Fujiyama, in Japan, is 259 feet tall, with an extremely steep 65-degree first drop.

Anton Schwarzkopf/Intamin, AG

German designer Anton Schwarzkopf, the principal designer for Intamin, AG, was also in the business of building amusement rides well before he made a big roller coaster splash in the 1960s, when he designed and manufactured what has become a very familiar sight at most smaller amusement parks and traveling carnivals. His Jet Star, Wild Cat, and Jumbo Jet compact portable steel models, most in the 50- to 60-foot height range, are still popular among roller coaster fans.

Jet Stars can be found at Casino Pier in Seaside Heights, New Jersey (at the very edge of the pier, right over the water), Morey's Pier in North Wildwood, New Jersey, and Indiana Beach in Monticello, Indiana (known as the Tig'rr). The ride is distinguished by its ground-hugging banked turns and four- to five-passenger single cars, in which riders sit in tandem.

Wild Cats feature single cars for four passengers, seated side by side. The most notable permanent installations of this type are at Cedar Point in Ohio

Laser, Dorney Park, a prime example of Anton Schwarzkopf's handiwork. (Courtesy of Dorney Park)

and at Bell's Amusement Park in Tulsa, Oklahoma (a slightly smaller version than the one in Ohio).

Jumbo Jets and their smaller brothers, City Jets and Jet Star II's, are distinguished by their spiraling lift-hills. Much rarer than Jet Stars or Wild Cats, all three feature tandem seating, usually with two or three cars linked together to form a train. A Jumbo Jet operates at Coney Island, Brooklyn, New York. There is a City Jet on Wonderland Pier in Ocean City, New Jersey. Jet Star II's operate at Lagoon in Farmington, Utah, and La Fería in Mexico City, where it is called Tornado.

Schwarzkopf began installing larger, permanent rides based on Jumbo Jets in the 1970s. Generically known as speed racers, they send four- or five-car trains with tandem seating along several thousand feet of twisting, turning track, all computer-designed to allow passengers to ride safely without the need for a lap-bar. Versions still in operation are the Whizzer at Six Flags Great America in Gurnee, Illinois, and Zambezi Zinger at Worlds of Fun in Kansas City, Missouri.

One of Anton Schwarzkopf's U.S. masterpieces is the triple-looping Mind Bender at Six Flags Over Georgia. (Courtesy of Bobby Nagy)

Not to be outdone by Arrow Dynamics, Schwarzkopf introduced a looping steel coaster in 1976. The Great American Revolution at Six Flags Magic Mountain in Valencia, California, was the first modern roller coaster to feature a 360-degree loop. Other Schwarzkopf looping coasters currently in operation are the Six Flags Over Georgia Mind Bender (still one of the world's best looping steel roller coasters), Shockwave at Six Flags Over Texas in Arlington, Laser at Dorney Park in Allentown, Pennsylvania, and Mindbender at Galaxyland in Edmonton, Alberta, Canada. Anton Schwarzkopf's looping coasters are distinguished by the fact that, although extremely smooth, they are designed with more wooden roller coaster attributes, like negative and lateral g's, and can operate with just a single lap-bar (although several also feature unnecessary over-the-shoulder harnesses). Some of the world's most intense looping steel roller coasters, such as the Thriller, Drier Looping, and Olympia Looping, are portable Schwarzkopf models that can be found at traveling European fairs.

Charles Dinn and Curtis Summers

Although Charles Dinn and Curtis Summers operated two separate companies, the Dinn Corporation and Curtis Summers, Inc., their collaborative efforts, with Dinn as the builder and Summers the designer, resulted in some of the great wooden roller coasters of our time.

Charlie Dinn burst onto the roller coaster scene in a huge way. He was responsible for building Paramount's Kings Island's Beast, which is still the longest wooden roller coaster ever built. After he formed the Dinn Corporation, his first projects involved moving older wooden coasters from parks that had closed to new parks that had purchased the rides. This task had rarely been attempted in the past, but Dinn changed all that. His relocation of the San Antonio, Texas, Rocket to Knoebel's Amusement Resort in Pennsylvania is considered miraculous. Dinn was also to work miracles with the Lakemont Park, Pennsylvania, Skyliner (moved from New York State) and the huge Giant Coaster, formerly located at Paragon Park outside of Boston, Massachusetts. The Giant, now known as the Wild One, is happily rolling along at Adventure World in Largo, Maryland, and is the tallest wooden coaster (98 feet) ever to be moved from one park to another.

Dinn first teamed up with Curtis Summers on a completely new design with the Wolverine Wildcat at Michigan's Adventure in Muskegon and the

The Beast, under construction. (Courtesy of Paramount's Kings Island)

Raging Wolf Bobs at Geauga Lake outside Cleveland, Ohio. The Bobs was inspired by the great classic Riverview Bobs, an early Prior and Church masterpiece in Chicago. Opened in 1988, the Raging Wolf Bobs was a rare throwback to 1920s roller coasters, and Dinn and Summers were soon swamped with orders for rambunctious wooden roller coasters. They would not disappoint their customers.

Over the next few years, Dinn and Summers would build several coasters that today rank among the best in operation. The Timber Wolf at Kansas City, Missouri's Worlds of Fun features amazing airtime; Hercules at Dorney Park in Allentown, Pennsylvania, boasts the world's longest wooden roller coaster drop, at 157 feet; and Mean Streak at Ohio's Cedar Point is the second-tallest woodie in the world.

Dinn and Summers created their masterpiece at Six Flags Over Texas in 1990. The Texas Giant has consistently ranked as the best wooden roller coaster in the world since its opening day. Wild, rambunctious, and radical, the Giant has all the best elements of every great wooden coaster wrapped into one stunning package.

William Cobb and Associates

Bill Cobb had been in the business of building coasters long before he branched out on his own. He had worked closely with John Allen on some of his masterpieces, providing the structural engineering for the Great American Scream Machine in Georgia and the Screamin' Eagle in Missouri, both for the Six Flags Company.

In 1975, Cobb was asked by Six Flags to examine the Coney Island Cyclone, which had temporarily ceased to operate. Six Flags was thinking of purchasing the 1927 ride and moving it to its Astroworld park in Houston, Texas. Cobb determined that, although work could be done to restore the 1927 classic for operation at its present location, it would be less expensive to build a completely new ride in Houston. Six Flags received permission to copy the Cyclone, and Cobb went to work designing a larger, faster version of the older ride for the new park. When the Texas Cyclone opened in 1976, it was hailed as the world's number one roller coaster. A mirror image of the original, it had larger and slightly steeper drops.

In 1983, Cobb was asked to build another Cyclone, this time for Riverside Park in Agawam, Massachusetts. Unfortunately, the park only had a small parcel of land to build the ride on, and it was determined that a very different ride would have to be designed. Since park owners also wanted a ride of at least 100 feet in height, Cobb had to design a roller coaster with severely steep drops and viciously tight, twisted turns. Revered by coaster

~~~~~~

Roller Coaster Fact: Bill Cobb, when questioned on the wildness of his design for the Riverside Cyclone, responded by saying, "I had gas the night before I thought that one up."

~~~~~~

fans as a true return to the masterworks of Prior and Church and Harry Traver, the Riverside Cyclone became Cobb's masterpiece.

Cobb went on to build Le Monstre at La Ronde in Montreal, Canada. A dual-track racing coaster, it features a lift height of 132 feet, making it the tallest racing coaster in the world.

Cobb's assistant, John Pierce, went out on his own upon Cobb's death in 1991. Pierce built four coasters before quickly retiring, the most notable being the Rattler at Six Flags Fiesta Texas in San Antonio. At 180 feet, it is the tallest wooden roller coaster in the world, although its maximum drop length is only 124 feet.

Batman—The Ride, a great example of an inverted coaster. (Courtesy of Six Flags Great Adventure)

Bolliger and Mabillard

Swiss designers and engineers Walter Bolliger and Claude Mabillard introduced their first coaster at Six Flags Great America in Illinois. Iron Wolf, a steel looping stand-up coaster, took the world by storm in 1990 because of its extreme smoothness.

In 1992, the company introduced a ride that made the entire amusement industry stand up and take notice. The inverted coaster featured ski-lift-style vehicles with trains of cars hanging below the track. The ride, also residing in Six Flags Great America, was capable of executing inversions, including several never before attempted, like heartline spins. Dubbed Batman—The Ride, the coaster was unlike anything ever created for an amusement park before. Larger versions soon appeared at Ohio's Cedar Point (Raptor) and both Busch Gardens parks, with Florida's Montu in stiff competition with Virginia's Alpengeist for the title of best of its type.

It was a project in 1993, however, that made B&M the steel coaster manufacturer most in demand throughout the world. Kumba, also at Busch Gardens in Florida, was not a new-fangled "gimmick" roller coaster. No dangling legs, no standing passengers. Kumba was a traditional sit-down looping steel roller coaster, basically the same concept that had been in use by parks for twenty years. Its extreme smoothness, outrageous new-style inversions, and sheer quality ensure the ride a top position on any top ten list, and B&M already has enough orders for their product to keep them busy into the next century.

Other B&M masterpieces currently in operation include Mantis, a huge and intense stand-up coaster at Cedar Point in Ohio, and Dragon Khan at Port Aventura in Spain, currently holding the world's record for number of inversions on a single roller coaster—a whopping eight!

Custom Coasters International

CCI is a family company, with strong roots in the coaster-building business. President Denise Dinn Larrick is the daughter of famed builder Charlie Dinn. Larrick's husband is vice president. Designers Larry Bill and Dennis McNulty create works that pay tribute to the great designers of the past.

When the company first started out, they were not interested in building the world's tallest anything for big-buck theme parks. Instead, they offered smaller, more affordable rides and marketed their product to the more intimate family-owned and -operated parks. This has caused a bit of a wooden coaster building boom, as parks that found previous manufacturers too cost-prohibitive could now get exactly the type of ride they wanted, and from exactly the type of people they wanted to do business with. Since 1992, the

Great Coasters International built the Wildcat at Hersheypark with coasters of the 1920s in mind. (Courtesy of Jennifer O'Rourke)

company has built over a dozen wooden coasters, all of varying sizes. Its masterpieces are Great White, a pier-dwelling oceanside thriller at Wild Wheels Pier on the New Jersey shore in Wildwood; Raven, an homage to dad Charles Dinn's Beast, located at Holiday World in Santa Claus (yes, you read that right), Indiana; and MegaFobia, a particularly wild ride located in Wales, Great Britain.

Great Coasters International

Designer Mike Boodley and builder Clair Hain left CCI and formed their own company in 1995. Their one project so far has been the Wildcat at Hersheypark in Pennsylvania. The Wildcat is a complete rethinking of the great rides of the 1920s. Chock-filled with Harry Traver spiral dips and Prior and Church banked turns, the Wildcat is a modern masterpiece based on classic designs, and it was an instant hit. Many more rides are on the horizon for these guys, and the coaster-riding public can't wait.

Vekoma International

Another manufacturer of roller coasters is Vekoma International, a company based in the Netherlands, which has used patents held by Arrow Dynamics and ideas from B&M to create affordable production models of some of the former companies' most popular rides. Vekoma is an extremely prolific supplier of coasters, and its suspended looping model is one of the most popular coaster installations worldwide, outdone in sales only by the Boomerang, another Vekoma product that is the most widely sold production-model coaster in the world.

S&MC

S&MC started out by supplying to parks a production model known as the Windstorm, basically designed to replace aging compact portable coasters in use as permanent installations. S&MC's highest-profile ride may well be the High Roller at the Stratosphere Tower in Las Vegas. Billed as the world's highest coaster (note—highest, not tallest), it resides on the *top* of the tower, spinning its guests through the course 900 feet above the ground. S&MC, along with Premier Rides, rocketed coasters into the twenty-first century with Outer Limits Flight of Fear, twin versions of which operate at Paramount's Kings Island (Ohio) and Paramount's Kings Dominion (Virginia). Both are enclosed rides, and their trains rocket out of the station by linear induction launch systems, speeding from 0 to 56 mph in just five short seconds. This technology eliminates the need for a lift-hill and provides passengers with an extremely intense ride experience.

D. H. Morgan Manufacturing

Dana Morgan, president of this new-kid-on-the-block company, also has a rich history of coaster building in his family: his dad was one of the founders of Arrow Dynamics and was partially responsible for the first steel coaster in the world, Disneyland's Matterhorn.

It is appropriate, then, that the younger Morgan has carved his niche in the coaster-building business by supplying to parks huge, mega-steel non-looping monsters. Taking up where Arrow left off, the company has built Wild Thing at Shakopee, Minnesota's Valleyfair! Family Amusement Park and Steel Force at Dorney Park in Pennsylvania. Both rides feature lift-hill heights of 200 feet.

DORNEY PARK'S STEEL FORCE IS BORN

A look into the development and construction of a roller coaster shows that building a new, multimillion-dollar thrill ride is a lot easier than one would think. Along with this ease come some unexpected detours and problems, however.

Take Steel Force, for example, the new-for-1997 mega-monster built by Dorney Park in Allentown, Pennsylvania. When Cedar Fair, LP, purchased Dorney in 1992, the first thing the company did was begin renovating and preparing the park, which had been in operation for over a century, so that large crowds drawn to the park by big, new attractions could be comfortably accommodated. Much "cosmetic" work was performed at the park, and today it looks better than ever, with new, wide midways and lush landscaping designed to make guests enjoy the amusement park experience all the more. The park lacked the usual "required" assortment of water rides (although Wildwater Kingdom is located right next door), so a river rapids ride and a giant splashdown chute were the major ride additions. These and other attractions geared toward families—and, specifically, children—made the park one of the best family entertainment centers on the East Coast of America.

Steel Force is the world's new number one steel roller coaster. (Courtesy of Dorney Park)

Also in the planning, for at least three years, was a roller coaster. Within one year, the park applied to the local town council for permission to build a large steel coaster, to reach breathtaking heights of more than 200 feet.

Soon the screaming started—not from riders on the magnificent new creation, but from residents living around the park, who believed that they could maintain a tranquil lifestyle while living next door to a major amusement park.

Not that the park causes any problems. New attractions could legally be built right up to the park's property line, but they never get closer than seventy feet. The park tries to be the best neighbor it possibly can be, building protective berms and planting tall trees, all at its own expense. A new entrance to the park was even built, redirecting guest traffic off of local streets in residential neighborhoods onto commercial boulevards nearer to major highways.

Still, several spoilsports complained, and the complaints caused delays. Park officials met with local residents and governments to diminish their fears, reminding them that the park had gone through the same controversy when it built Hercules, at the time the tallest wooden coaster in the world, and a ride that had never caused noise or traffic problems within the community.

Finally, approval came. The park then contracted with D. H. Morgan Manufacturing to construct a non-looping steel scream machine, similar in style to the Magnum XL-200 and Wild Thing, in operation at two other Cedar Fair parks.

Dorney Park rests within a small valley, and it was decided, again for the benefit of the neighbors, that the new coaster would stretch along the section of the park located at the lowest point in the terrain, so that it would be as obscure as a 200-foot-tall roller coaster could possibly be.

The final design, layout, and profile were all completed in late 1996, and site clearing began that September. Once the area for a coaster has been cleared, concrete footings are the first signs of construction. Coaster footings, which provide the solid foundation for the structure, reach from just above the surface of the ground to as much as 75 feet below it. Footings for Steel Force reach from one end of the park to the other and negotiate a hillside, at one point also crossing a creek.

Coaster structure does not go up piece by piece, as one might think. In the case of wooden coasters, precut wood is assembled on the ground, then lifted by crane, and fitted into place. These sections are anchored by bolts to the footings, and to each other. In the case of a steel coaster like Steel Force, Morgan Manufacturing prefabricated all sections of the structure and track at their California plant, then shipped the pieces to Dorney, thousands of miles away.

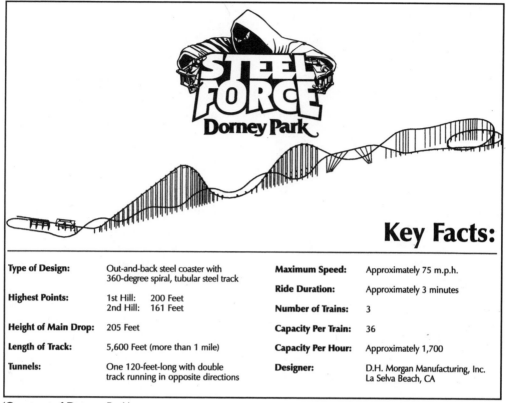

Key Facts:

Type of Design:	Out-and-back steel coaster with 360-degree spiral, tubular steel track	**Maximum Speed:**	Approximately 75 m.p.h.
		Ride Duration:	Approximately 3 minutes
Highest Points:	1st Hill: 200 Feet 2nd Hill: 161 Feet	**Number of Trains:**	3
Height of Main Drop:	205 Feet	**Capacity Per Train:**	36
Length of Track:	5,600 Feet (more than 1 mile)	**Capacity Per Hour:**	Approximately 1,700
Tunnels:	One 120-feet-long with double track running in opposite directions	**Designer:**	D.H. Morgan Manufacturing, Inc. La Selva Beach, CA

(Courtesy of Dorney Park)

Like a giant erector set, a section of steel would be lifted by crane, bolted into place, and presto, it's done! Huge 30-foot sections of track are then lifted into place and bolted to the structure. On each section of track, one end is hollow, and the other end has an extension on it, so the adjoining pieces fit into each other like a key into a lock, forming a smooth, continuous track for forthcoming trains to glide over. A major section of the ride could be completed in a matter of days.

The structure, once completed, is fitted with computer sensors (to provide blocking capabilities, a safety feature that forestalls collisions by preventing two trains from operating in the circuit at the same time). A lift-chain is installed to carry the multi-ton train and its passengers to the apex of the first hill. Painting of the structure has been done before construction, but touch-ups are often necessary. The station, queue lines, and landscaping are then completed, while the computer-controlled operating console is installed.

Once the trains have been added to the track, testing begins. First, the cars are weight-loaded with sandbags, and when the new train has completed a circuit (in Steel Force's case, the train flew through the entire course on its first run), human "sandbags" volunteer to be the first passengers. (These are usually members of the construction company or park personnel; members of the public can't volunteer for the job, although there are many who would love to!) A media day and grand opening was held to introduce the ride and create a frenzied faction of the public, all of whom just couldn't wait to experience the full force of Steel Force.

The quality of engineering and magnificence of the design made it apparent very quickly that Steel Force was the world's new number one steel roller coaster. No other ride provides the gravity forces, from extreme negative to extreme positive, that this one does. No other ride provides such a smooth, yet wild experience. And only a very select group of rides have the type of exquisite pacing that make the final moments every bit as good as the first big drops.

Steel Force does all of this, and then some. It's not only the longest, tallest, and fastest coaster in the eastern U.S., it's also the best. So, how about a ride on this baby?

3 GETTING THE MOST WHEN YOU COAST

You might think that roller coastering is a simple endeavor. Go to the park, wait on the line, ride the ride, and move on to the next.

Well, you can certainly do it that way, and you'll probably enjoy yourself just fine. But there are shortcuts and tricks of the trades that we "professionals" have been using for years to get maximum enjoyment from our park trips.

Follow these tips and you'll get more rides, wait in line less time, and enhance your ride experience. In short, you'll enjoy riding roller coasters much more.

RAINY DAYS SHOULDN'T GET YOU DOWN

Parks are much, much less crowded when it rains, or even when it looks like rain. To avoid lines, plan to go to the parks when the sun doesn't look like it's going to make an appearance, because the absence of the sun will also bring with it the absence of thousands of people as well. If that isn't enough, roller coasters with wet tracks run much faster than they normally do when dry. Be warned, however, that some parks do not operate coasters in even the slightest rain, and no park runs any tall ride at all when rain is accompanied by lightning. (The words "human lightning rod" come to mind.) Also keep in mind that small crowds and a faster-running roller coaster are a trade-off for being soaked to the skin. And a driving rain hitting your face while you're traveling at 60 mph may not be the most pleasurable thing you'll ever experience.

IT DOES MATTER WHERE YOU SIT—AND HOW!

Most parks let you sit in whatever seat you choose to on a roller coaster. In these cases, the front and back seats will always have longer lines than any other seat. Contrary to what some people will tell you, it does matter where

The classic Thunder Hawk.
(Courtesy of Dorney Park)

you sit. Certain rides are better in the front; others, in back. Generally, a roller coaster is smoother in the front, much snappier in the back. The middle of the train neutralizes the extremes felt at either end, offering not much more than a fast trip along the track.

The front of a roller coaster train tends to "hang" down the drops, as it is being held back by the rear of the train. However, it is pushed quite severely up the hills and through inversions, enabling passengers to feel more extreme forces of gravity. If you require an unobstructed view of the track, sit in the front seat. (Seat number two will not even come close to providing the same visual, so don't settle for it if the front-seat line is too long.) If your reason for sitting in the front is to experience the extreme g-forces, as well as negative g's (those delicious moments where your body lifts off the seat and you become weightless), only sit in the front if there's no line. While the negative g's are fine in the front seat, they are even more accentuated in the third seat (this applies only to non-looping wood and steel coasters).

The back of a train will be yanked down each drop, enabling those sitting in the rear to experience the full force and length of the drop. (This is the effect that causes some people to think the back of the train "goes faster" than the front, which is impossible, of course—the back of a coaster train has never been known to return to the station before the front of a train!) Passengers in the rear, depending on the severity of the design, tend to be catapulted out of the seat on the drop, making the ride generally much wilder than in any other place on the train. The back seat is the most severe, but if the line is too long, the one right in front of it is usually almost as good.

Wherever you choose to sit—front, back, or middle—whether or not you sit directly over the wheels also determines the nature of your ride. Each coaster train is usually comprised of from three to seven cars. Each car will either have two seats (seating four passengers total), or three seats (seating six). Each individual car has four wheels, two in front and two in back, which ride above the rails and enable the train to roll forward. Sitting in the rear seat of the car (third on three-bench cars, second on two-bench) will result in a rougher ride. Not only are you directly above the wheels that are making contact with the track, there is nothing solid behind your seat to act as a shock absorber (additional cars linked to the rear of your car will not serve this purpose). If that's what you want, have at it. But if you're looking for a smoother ride, choose the seat over the front wheels or, in the case of three-bench cars, the middle seat, which is not over wheels at all. Your teeth won't rattle, but you'll still feel all the gravity forces.

Wherever you sit, how you sit will also affect your ride. If you like to hold your hands in the air, go right ahead. Keep in mind, though, that holding your arms up forces you to stiffen your body somewhat; this may make you fight against the natural flow of the ride. Try sitting with your body relaxed (for some, this won't be an easy thing to do). Let your hands rest on the lap-bar, or hold on lightly. You'll really get the experience of whatever ride you're on.

TO SEE OR NOT TO SEE

If you're afraid—whatever you do, DO NOT CLOSE YOUR EYES!!! What you can't see is much scarier than what you can see, and riding a roller coaster with your eyes closed will only make the experience all the more terrifying. (This works in reverse for serious thrill seekers. If you want to make the ride more frightening, just close your eyes.) You won't be able to see the hills, twists, or loops coming, and your body won't be able to register what's happening until it's too late. Not being able to anticipate is what makes even the most mild indoor-in-the-dark or backward coaster so intense.

Roller Coaster Fact: Among the lost items found beneath roller coasters—in addition to the expected wallets, loose change, and keys—have been several rather mysterious curiosities such as a glass eye, a prosthetic leg, brassieres, and more false teeth than could possibly be imagined. Strangely enough, many of these items remain unclaimed by their owners.

FACING BACKWARD

Some parks have coasters that feature trains facing backward on the track. All steel shuttle loop coasters must traverse the course backward to return to their station starting points, but there are also wooden racing coasters that have one side forward, one backward. Going backward, you will experience all the forces that are part of the forward coastering experience, but you will feel them quite differently. (An example: forward inertia will push the rider back into his seat going forward—backward, the rider will be pushed away from the seat.) Keep in mind that since none of the course will be visible to you, a backward ride will be more physical and somewhat scarier, as we just discussed above.

WHAT DO I RIDE FIRST?

Try to arrive at the park just before the gates open. If you're not familiar with the park's layout, get a map (either handed to you at the parking toll booth, or available at the main entrance ticket booth). Take a few minutes to find the roller coasters you want to ride. When the gates open, unless you really *must* ride the roller coaster nearest the front gate, head for the coaster that is furthest away. Most people go immediately to whatever major attraction is closest, so you'll have at least a few rides without any lines before others start to show up. By afternoon, you'll find the shortest lines of the day on the rides close to the entrance, as by that time the crowds have moved on further into the park. You'll also find that just before park closing, rides further from the front gate will have the shortest lines.

When a park opens a new roller coaster, or any big, splashy new attraction, by all means go to the park. If you can wait to ride the new ride until a later date, you just might find yourself with no lines to wait on at all for anything else. Almost everyone will be queued up to ride the new attraction.

Always check to see how many trains are running on a roller coaster before you wait in line. If the particular coaster you want to ride is only running one train, check back later. A long line with two or three trains running moves much swifter than a shorter line with only one train. Of course, if there's no line at all, it doesn't matter.

Some pay-one-price parks allow you to reride without exiting and reentering the line. This happens only when there is no line, and no one is waiting for your seat. Since people will always queue up for the front or back seats, sitting nearer the middle of the train will probably ensure you more rides without having to get off the train and walk around. If the park does not offer this policy, you'll have no choice but to exit at the end of your ride; the attendants didn't make the rules, and therefore cannot bend them.

Call the park to find out if any large group outings are scheduled for the day of your visit. (You can usually get this information several days ahead.) Large groups may mean thousands of children, and most of them love roller coasters and will be standing on "your" line.

ATTENTION COASTERING PARENTS WITH SMALL CHILDREN

The minimum height restriction on adult coasters usually ranges from 42 to 54 inches, which prohibits most young children from riding. These height restrictions are determined by the type of restraints contained in the vehicle, as well as the nature of the ride itself. They are always strictly enforced.

Many parks have child-size roller coasters that allow adults to ride if accompanied by kids. Most parks offer a "parent swap" program for couples and families who wish to ride an adult coaster but do not have non-riding adults to leave their children with. One adult rides the coaster while the other waits at the exit of the ride with the kids. When the first adult has ridden, he or she switches places with the one who first stayed with the little ones, affording both adults a ride without waiting in line two separate times. This policy is typically not made widely known, and the logistics may vary from park to park, so check with Guest Services regarding the exact policy in effect at the park before you attempt to ride in this manner.

HANDICAPPED POLICIES

Most parks offer special services for physically challenged guests. These days, amusement rides are generally wheelchair accessible and available to most guests, depending on what the individual's disability may be. Don't attempt to ride before you've checked on what rules and regulations may be in effect at the park you're visiting. You can get this information from Guest Services, and you may want to call ahead for it.

THEME PARKS CAN BE EXPENSIVE . . .

. . . unless you play your cards right. Try to buy your tickets in advance through AAA or other sources. There's usually a small discount.

Some parks offer two day tickets at considerable savings. If you plan on visiting a park more than twice in a season, your best bet would be to purchase a season pass. Season passes often sell for a price less than the amount it would cost to visit the park in question twice. Additionally, season pass holders are often invited to exclusive parties at the park, and may receive discount coupons good for free visits, discounted merchandise, etc.

Several theme park companies now also offer the option of using a season pass purchased at one park at all other parks they own and operate, for free admission. A Six Flags pass purchased at any Six Flags park is good for use at all Six Flags Theme Parks. Paramount Parks offers the same deal. Cedar Fair, LP, owns four parks (Cedar Point, Sandusky, Ohio; Valleyfair! Family Theme Park, Shakopee, Minnesota; Dorney Park and Wildwater Kingdom, Allentown, Pennsylvania; and Worlds of Fun/Oceans of Fun in Kansas City, Missouri) and allows admission to all of them with one park's season pass. Premier Parks currently owns Frontier City and White Water Bay (Oklahoma City, Oklahoma), Adventure World (Largo, Maryland), Geauga Lake (Aurora, Ohio), Wyandot Lake (Columbus, Ohio), Darien Lake (Corfu, New York), the Great Escape (Lake George, New York), Elitch Gardens (Denver, Colorado), and Riverside Park (Agawam, Massachusetts), plus several water parks; all can be entered by using a season pass purchased at any one of the parks.

Busch Gardens does not currently offer free admission to holders of season passes from other parks within the chain, but does offer certain discounts on parking and merchandise.

OBSERVE ALL RULES OF THE GAME

Do not attempt to stand up when riding, or engage in any other unsafe activities. If you do, the park will eject you from its property, at the very least. You might find yourself in even more hot water, as in some places it is a misdemeanor crime to engage in unsafe practices on amusement devices. Of course, the worst possible outcome—that you or others could be hurt or killed—in itself should be the key reason to abide by all riding rules. If you feel that the roller coaster isn't thrilling enough unless you attempt to stand up or commit other foolish acts, then maybe coaster riding isn't for you, and you need to find something else to do with your time.

4 TYPES OF ROLLER COASTERS

Roller coasters come in all different shapes, sizes, and varieties. In this chapter, you can familiarize yourself with the different types of rides you'll be encountering in subsequent pages, as well as on trips to the actual parks.

WOOD

Wooden roller coasters have been operating in the United States since 1884. Not much has changed in ensuing years—the ride is still a somewhat simple concept and doesn't offer any high-tech variations at all. Yet purists will tell you wood is what roller coastering is all about. While steel coasters come in many different varieties, there are just two wood variations. The reason for this is either because steel is capable of more acrobatics, or because wood is capable of accomplishing its goals without the gimmicks that steel relies on.

While some wood coasters are dual-tracked racing versions and some feature trains facing backward on the track, the two major different types of wood coaster are as follows.

• *Twister* Spaghetti-bowl in nature, usually featuring criss-crossing trackage, many turns, and steep drops. Fans of wooden twisters point out that this type of ride offers more surprises than out and backs, with hidden drops and sudden turns.

• *Out and back* Very simple in layout, basically starting out at point A, moving to point B, and returning to point A. Dual-track racing coasters are commonly designed as out and backs. A variation on the standard out and back is the double out and back, which moves from A to B, back to A, then back to B, and finishes at A.

Thunder Hawk, Dorney Park. (Courtesy of Dorney Park)

STEEL

• *Looping*   Any standard (trains riding above the track, with passengers sitting in a normal position) roller coaster that goes upside down.

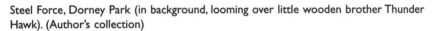

Roller Coaster Fact: The Viper at Six Flags Magic Mountain
in Valencia, California, at 188 feet, is the world's tallest looping steel roller coaster, although the Steel Phantom at Kennywood (near Pittsburgh, Pennsylvania), with a drop of 225
feet down a mountainside, offers the longest steel looping
drop and the fastest speed.

• *Non-looping* Usually large, standard rides that do not feature any
upside-down elements.

• *Inverted* Looping coaster with trains hanging below the track.
Passengers sit in ski-lift-type vehicles, their legs dangling below them in the
open air.

• *Suspended* Non-looping ride with enclosed trains hanging below the
track. Suspended coaster trains swing freely with each turn; inverted coaster
trains do not.

• *Stand-up* A coaster with vehicles designed to accommodate passengers in a standing, upright position; usually looping.

Steel Force, Dorney Park (in background, looming over little wooden brother Thunder
Hawk). (Author's collection)

- *Mine Train*   Family-type themed ride, with trains resembling loco-motives or mining cars. Mine trains are big on small drops and lots of twists and turns.
- *Bobsled*   Single cars or trains running freely inside a trough, just like a real bobsled.
- *Shuttle*   Any coaster that returns backward along the same track, whether in a straight line or in a course with many twists and turns. Shuttles usually have inversions.
- *Compact Portable*   Any type of small, traveling roller coaster, com-monly with cars for one, two, or four passengers. Many parks offer such rides as permanent attractions, even though they can be easily moved.

There are also several variations of roller coasters that can be constructed of wood or steel.

- *Terrain*   Rides that use the topography of the earth to dictate their layouts and profiles; found in parks with hills, ravines, mountains, etc.
- *Junior*   Rides that are not quite as large as their adult, full-size ver-sions, but not necessarily small enough to be considered strictly for children. Not to be confused with steel compact portables, although they are often similar in size.
- *Kiddie*   Small coasters designed for children, although adults are frequently welcome to ride, if they can fit into the child-size cars.

5 THE TEN BEST WOOD COASTERS IN THE WORLD

1. TEXAS GIANT

Six Flags Over Texas, Arlington, Texas

The world's number one roller coaster made its debut in March 1990. It's been the park's number one ride ever since. This masterpiece of mayhem has a 143-foot-tall lift-hill that leads riders into an absolute maelstrom of twists and dives that are unequaled by any other amusement device, wood, steel or otherwise! In the years since this ultimate ride came on the scene, sections of it that were deemed a little too intense have been redesigned. Still, this bucking bronco, although somewhat tamer, but markedly faster, remains without peer. In fact, each year, it becomes an even more fine-tuned terror inducer. Don't miss it.

Roller Coaster Fact: The oldest wooden roller coaster still operating is the Jack Rabbit at Clementon Lake Park in Clementon, New Jersey, built in 1919 and still in its original location. The oldest steel coaster is Disneyland's Matterhorn, which opened in 1959.

The best roller coaster in the whole universe, the Texas Giant at Six Flags Over Texas. (Courtesy of Bobby Nagy)

2. CYCLONE

Astroland (at Coney Island), Brooklyn, New York

This is the original 1927 Coney Island masterpiece. Its 85-foot-tall first drop at a 60-degree angle still sends shock waves of fright through its riders. The Cyclone probably has the best combination of steep drops, wild turns, and surprises of any roller coaster currently operating.

3. GREAT WHITE

Wild Wheels Pier, Wildwood, New Jersey

Built in 1996, the Great White is a reincarnation of 1920s-style oceanside coasters, both in design and setting. A full two-thirds of the ride is built directly over the Wildwood beach's sand, and the ride's many pleasures begin with a 25-foot drop immediately out of the station, into a tunnel under the pier. At 57 degrees, the ride contains one of the steepest after-lift-hill main drops in the world. Relentless pacing makes this ride a must.

~~~~~~

Roller Coaster Fact: The late Ruth Voss, for many years director of public relations at what is now known as Paramount's Kings Island, was afflicted with arthritis. She found that a ride on the Beast each morning "loosened her up" and alleviated much of the stiffness associated with the disease.

~~~~~~

4. BEAST

Paramount's Kings Island, Cincinnati, Ohio

The longest wooden roller coaster in the world, and one of the fastest. At 7,400 feet, this ride consists of two large drops, one into an underground tunnel, the other into a 540-degree helix. The Beast is built on thirty-five acres (as large as some entire parks!) of hilly terrain, and most of the ride is constructed low to the ground, its undulations dictated by the earth's surface itself. A ride on this monster lasts almost four minutes—nearly twice the ride time of most other roller coasters. A legend since the day it opened.

5. COMET

The Great Escape, Lake George, New York

This 96-foot-high ride originally opened at Crystal Beach Park, on the Canadian shores of Lake Erie near Buffalo, New York. When that park closed in 1989, Charles Wood, owner of the Great Escape, purchased and moved this classic. Reopened in 1994, the rebuilt Comet proved to be an even better coaster than it was in its original home. A double out-and-back-design, it features a constant speed and the best and most abundant airtime of any roller coaster in the world. The Comet is 4,000 feet of total, wild abandonment.

6. GEORGIA CYCLONE

Six Flags Over Georgia, Atlanta, Georgia

In the mid-1970s, the Six Flags family of theme parks wanted to purchase the original Coney Island Cyclone and move it to Six Flags Astroworld in Houston, Texas. For financial reasons, they decided to ask permission to build a replica instead. The result was the Texas Cyclone, a larger, faster, and wilder version of the original. A full fourteen years later, and after much taming of the Houston copy, the company built its second Cyclone at its Georgia facility; two others followed in other Six Flags parks. None of the copies come close to the level of intensity of the Brooklyn one and only, but this southern version approaches the wildness of its namesake. Judged on its own merits, the Georgia Cyclone is one of the best kick-butt roller coasters on the planet. Its "slammer" qualities on each of its steep hills are among the best in the business.

7. SCREAMIN' EAGLE

Six Flags St. Louis, Allenton, Missouri

Famed roller coaster designer John Allen came out of retirement to build this hillside beauty; at the time of its 1976 opening, it was the longest (3,872 feet), tallest (110 feet), and fastest (70 mph) roller coaster in the world. While it no longer carries that status, the Eagle is still one of the world's great coasters. The ride sits along a ridge at the back and highest point of this hillside park, providing a breathtaking backdrop. The ride itself uses its uneven terrain to its best advantage. Its third drop is deeper than its first, and large drops continue right up to the end. New trains added in the 1990s made the ride faster and more intense.

8. MEAN STREAK

Cedar Point, Sandusky, Ohio

When this ride opened in 1991, it was the tallest wooden roller coaster in the world (161 feet). It lost that status the following year to the Rattler (Six Flags Fiesta Texas, in San Antonio), which topped out at 180 feet. Rattler's 171-foot-long drop proved to be more than the park could handle, and subsequent rebuilding resulted in a 180-foot-tall structure with a drop descending only 125 feet, pushing the Mean Streak back into the world's tallest category once again. Mean Streak was "inspired" by the Texas Giant, and while the two share certain design similarities, this larger brother is not quite as wild. Still, a fast, twisting ride over more than one mile of track puts it near the top of the heap.

9. GRIZZLY

Paramount's Kings Dominion, Doswell, Virginia

This has got to be one of the sneakiest roller coasters in the world. It was completely hidden in the woods until just a few seasons ago, when the park began clearing land for expansion purposes. Approaching from the park's entrance still leaves this ride shrouded in mystery, however, and even from the station not much can be detected. Once on the ride, there's still trickery afoot. Grizzly's first drop, a twisting 85-footer, is comparatively mild, and immediately following that, the ride has an extremely slow, flat turn. At this moment, most passengers are thinking how they just wasted forty-five minutes in line, but then "Grizz" shifts into overdrive, becoming one of the wildest, most action-packed rides you'd ever encounter. Along the way, passengers are treated to a hidden tunnel that most assuredly appears too small for the train to fit into. Based on a defunct 1920s classic, Grizzly is perhaps the greatest use of psychology in roller coaster design.

10. RIVERSIDE CYCLONE

Riverside Park, Agawam, Massachusetts

Another coaster inspired by 1920s classics—in this case, however, no single design, but insane elements indicative of the style most prevalent during that time, and exaggerated in concept, to boot. This park wanted a ride of a certain height but only had a small parcel of land available to build on, so designer Bill Cobb was forced to make each drop treacherously steep and the turns truly wicked. The ride's crowning glory is its first drop, which consists of an awesome 200-degree turn *during* a super-steep modified double-dropping hill! It's the most intense, wildest piece of roller coaster trackage today, and perhaps ever built.

Also Worth Mentioning

• RAVEN, Holiday World, Santa Claus, Indiana.   A very intense terrain ride, sort of a miniature Beast, but in some ways an improvement on its larger cousin.

• WILDCAT, Hersheypark, Hershey, Pennsylvania.   A 1990s-built ride that is a direct descendent of 1920s classics, in that all of its hills are located in its turns, and vice versa.

• WHITE CYCLONE, Nagashima Spaland, Mei-ken, Japan.   A huge, extremely fast ride, with two reverse-direction helices. Only the second wooden roller coaster ever built in Japan.

• MEGAFOBIA, Oakwood Leisure Park, Pembrokeshire, Wales, Great Britain.   Great Britain's largest and most intense wood coaster features one of the steepest first drops in the world, followed by a twisted knot of wood track, which is almost impossible to follow without a map.

• THUNDERBOLT, Kennywood Park, West Mifflin, Pennsylvania. Originally built in 1924 as the Pippin, and modified in 1968 to include more hills, the Thunderbolt utilizes a hillside and has two final drops approaching 100 feet in height.

• CYCLONE, Lakeside Amusement Park, Denver, Colorado. A rare combination of a twister and an out and back, with a heart-stopping spiral plunge into a veritable spaghetti bowl of twisting, churning track.

Roller Coaster Fact: The Coney Island Cyclone, although a wooden roller coaster, has a mostly steel structure, because local ordinances prohibited the building of wood structures beyond a certain height.

6 THE TEN BEST STEEL COASTERS IN THE WORLD

1. STEEL FORCE

Dorney Park, Allentown, Pennsylvania

A huge, non-looping steel coaster, similar in design to Cedar Point's Magnum XL-200. A 205-foot long drop into an underground tunnel is just the beginning for this ride—the longest, tallest, and fastest roller coaster on the East Coast. "The Force" stretches the entire length of the park and provides a lovely scenic tour of the park's three other adult roller coasters: it also passes within several feet of the first drops of the two wooden coasters in the park. No other ride in the world does what this one does, and it does it free of the usual steel coaster gimmickry like loops, dangling feet, standing positions, etc. In fact, despite its enormous size and its total steel construction, Steel Force offers all the attributes of a magnificently paced, classically designed wooden roller coaster.

2. ALPENGEIST

Busch Gardens, Williamsburg, Virginia

This is one of the finest steel coasters currently in operation, and one of the most terrifying. It is one of the new "inverted" models, which have only been around since 1992; their chair-lift-style vehicles hang below the track, enhanc-

~~~~~~

Roller Coaster Fact: Only seven full-circuit roller coasters currently operating reach a height 200 feet or more: Magnum XL-200, at Cedar Point; the Pepsi Max Big One, at Blackpool Pleasure Beach; Desperado, at Buffalo Bill's Resort and Casino; Wild Thing, at Valleyfair!; Fujiyama, in Japan; Manhattan Express, part of the New York New York Resort and Casino; and Steel Force, at Dorney Park. All are constructed of steel. Only Manhattan Express features inversion elements.

~~~~~~

ing the passenger's sense of flying. This mountain ghost is 195 feet tall, with a 17-story first drop, absolutely huge looping elements, and amazing speed. The ride is built at the edge of a ravine, into which it travels deeper and deeper with each inversion. For its grand finale, Alpengeist treats passengers to a few ground-hugging moments where it would be best if riders were not wearing platform shoes. Bolliger and Mabillard's newest masterpiece.

3. MONTU

Busch Gardens, Tampa, Florida

Although all previous inverted coasters caused sensations, this one took the best features of each and rolled them all into one: lightning-quick pacing like Batman—The Ride, the original inverted (Six Flags theme parks' signature ride); huge size (150 feet tall) like Raptor at Cedar Point; and underground tunnels like those featured on Nemesis, located at Alton Towers in England. The g-forces experienced on Montu may be among the most that extreme roller coaster riding will permit.

4. KUMBA

Busch Gardens, Tampa, Florida

This was truly the ride that cemented B&M's position as the number one steel coaster manufacturer in the world. While the company established itself by developing the inverted coaster and perfecting the stand-up coaster, Kumba was their first attempt at a type of ride that had been around for years: a standard, sit-down, above-the-track looping steel roller coaster. Kumba never lets up. The ride is beyond smooth and features inversion

One of the best steel coasters is Montu, Busch Gardens, Tampa. (Courtesy of Bobby Nagy)

elements that the "other" guys wouldn't have even attempted to try. Riders are always stunned when, as the Kumba train is about to enter its fourth huge inversion element, the train seems to pick up even more speed than it displayed previously. An absolute masterpiece.

5. MANTIS

Cedar Point, Sandusky, Ohio

A monumental stand-up coaster, enormous in size, and featuring pushed-to-the-limit intensity. A track layout that is so snarled and twisted it cannot be followed from the ground is only one of the many pleasures of this ultimate thrill ride. Novice riders may want to get a few more "tamer" rides under their belts before venturing aboard this one. Yet another B&M winner.

6. RAPTOR

Cedar Point, Sandusky, Ohio

B&M strikes again with this large inverted coaster. Raptor's best features come from its having to be designed around existing structures on the park's midway, so that strange little twists and what can best be described as "lane changes" constantly fake out the passenger. Raptor's finest moment comes right at the beginning, with a first drop laid out as an elongated S-turn, heading into a sudden drop-off (best experienced in the back row on the right side) that provides the best sense of free-fall on any currently operating roller coaster.

7. MAGNUM XL-200

Cedar Point, Sandusky, Ohio

Of historic importance, as this was the first full-circuit roller coaster to top 200 feet in height (205 to be exact). Also noteworthy because it does not go upside down even once, although it was built at a time when all other parks were racing each other to construct giant steel coasters with more loops than their competition. Magnum offers a more traditional coaster experience, albeit of the giant-size variety. The slowest speed on this ride is faster than the fastest speed on the park's oldest coaster, 1964's Blue Streak.

8. BATMAN—THE RIDE

Six Flags Great Adventure, Jackson, New Jersey
Six Flags Great America, Gurnee, Illinois
Six Flags Magic Mountain, Valencia, California
Six Flags Over Georgia, Atlanta, Georgia
Six Flags St. Louis, Allenton, Missouri

The amusement industry was rocked off its foundation in 1992, when B&M debuted its first inverted roller coaster, Batman—The Ride, at Six Flags Great America. The ride caused a sensation among parkgoers as well, and while other parks clamored to sign contracts for their own versions, Six Flags began adding exact replicas to each of its own parks, first Great Adventure, then Magic Mountain, and so on. Themed to the long-popular Batman character, and more specifically to the current Batman motion picture series, Batman number one, two, and five feature identical track layouts, although the theming varies slightly from park to park. The St. Louis version, however, is a mirror image of the other four, offering a familiar yet completely different experience.

Roller Coaster Fact: Batman—The Ride at Six Flags Great America (Illinois) was the first roller coaster ever built that required special rules regarding riders' shoes.

9. MIND BENDER

Six Flags Over Georgia, Atlanta, Georgia

While all the other rides on this list were built in the late 1980s or early 1990s, Mind Bender came on the scene in 1978, making it an antique of sorts. This old-timer is far from ready for retirement, however. In fact, it was recently rethemed to include elements from the Batman movies. Designed by Anton Schwarzkopf, considered by many to be the father of the steel roller coaster, this ride is so precisely designed and so perfectly engineered that passengers tackle its two upside-down loops without the need for over-the-shoulder harnesses. A simple lap-bar is all you get on the Mind Bender, and it's all you need, as gravity holds you firmly to your seat at all times. There's nothing quite like this ride; long may she roll.

10. STEEL PHANTOM

Kennywood, West Mifflin, Pennsylvania

The tallest looping roller coaster in the world, as well as the fastest full-circuit coaster. The ride's first drop, a 160-foot twisting plunge, is nothing compared to its second drop—a 225-foot-high plummet down the side of a mountain at a 65-degree angle. Phantom has been known to approach speeds of 90 mph and represents intense coastering at its best.

Also Worth Mentioning

• TOP GUN, Paramount's Kings Island, Cincinnati, Ohio.   A suspended coaster, freely swinging its way through the course, on a structure built over and in a ravine. At times this ride can be terrifying, as its speed becomes relentless and the train swings to narrowly avoid support posts. The best of its kind in the world.

• GREAT NOR'EASTER, Morey's Pier, North Wildwood, New Jersey.   This is a suspended looping coaster, with passengers riding ski-lift-style seating. The installation of this ride is what makes it spectacular. Situated on an oceanside pier already jammed to the hilt with other rides and attractions, the Nor'Easter winds over, under, and through the other rides, providing passengers with the uneasy feeling that their shoes might go home with the people riding the extremely nearby log flume!

• FUJIYAMA, Fujikyu Highlands, Osaka, Japan.   The world's tallest full-circuit roller coaster. Like Magnum and Steel Force, Fuji doesn't go upside down at all; unlike those two, which are out and backs, Fuji is designed as a twister—and not just any twister. Apparently, the Coney Island Cyclone, the grandfather of all roller coasters, served as inspiration for this 265-foot-tall monster.

• DESPERADO, Buffalo Bill's Resort and Casino, Stateline, Nevada. A roller coaster without an amusement park. This giant, non-looping ride is built within and around a casino in the Nevada desert.

• CHANG, Kentucky Kingdom, Louisville, Kentucky. A slightly larger version of Cedar Point's Mantis, featuring one additional inversion, but lacking the spaghetti-bowl nature of its almost-twin.

• NEMESIS, Alton Towers, Staffordshire, England. An extravagantly themed inverted, from B&M, with many underground tunnels as its major attraction.

7 THE TEN PARKS WITH THE BEST ROLLER COASTER COLLECTIONS

1. CEDAR POINT

Sandusky, Ohio

When it comes to roller coasters, this park doesn't fool around. It has twelve of them, the most of any park in the world. But it's not just the number of coasters that should make this park any roller coaster lover's ultimate destination. The park also has the distinction of featuring at least one of almost every variety of coaster, and some of those in operation here were the longest, tallest, and fastest of their kind when first opened (and, in some cases, still are).

Most important, all the coasters at Cedar Point are not what might be considered total thrill machines, and that makes this collection especially perfect for family members who might not all share the same threshold for thrills. Not everyone has the desire to dive 200 feet down at 72 mph, so the Point offers rides for those folks, too. In fact, a small child beginning his or her coaster-riding life at Cedar Point could start out on the park's kiddie coaster and "graduate" to the next level each year as height or bravery allows.

Roller Coaster Fact: Gemini, at Cedar Point in Ohio, has the highest passenger capacity of any roller coaster in the world. With two tracks running three trains each, the ride can thrill 3,000 riders per hour.

Eight (count 'em, eight!) of Cedar Point's twelve roller coasters are visible in the bird's-eye view of the world's roller coaster capital. (Courtesy of Dan Feicht)

2. SIX FLAGS MAGIC MOUNTAIN

Valencia, California

The Six Flags Company is the largest operator of roller coasters in the world, with approximately sixty total of all shapes and sizes in eight theme parks worldwide. Ten of them are at this Southern California theme park.

This collection tends to be more thrill-ride oriented but families will find a few suitable to their level as well. The variety and quality of roller coasters here establish Six Flags Magic Mountain as the park with the best collection of thrilling rides in the western United States.

3. PARAMOUNT'S KINGS ISLAND

Cincinnati, Ohio

This is the park familiar to fans of early *Brady Bunch* episodes. The racing coaster that Mike, Carol, and the kids rode back in 1973 has been joined by eight others in the ensuing years. In fact, the Racer is widely credited as being the roller coaster that began a renaissance of sorts for coasters; after it opened, parks began building big wooden coasters in numbers that hadn't been seen since the 1920s. This collection today offers thrills, family adventures, and several one-of-a-kind experiences.

4. PARAMOUNT CANADA'S WONDERLAND

Vaughan, Ontario

The eight rolling rides here comprise the largest collection of coasters in Canada. They offer a mixed variety of thrills, from mild to wild. The two adult wooden coasters at the park were based on designs of coasters from a long-gone park in Cincinnati, Ohio.

5. SIX FLAGS OVER GEORGIA

Atlanta, Georgia

This seven-ride collection of roller coasters is a rather straightforward bunch, with not much unusual high-tech gimmickry available. The offerings here are, for the most part, more traditional up and down—or up, upside down, and down—but what distinguishes these rides is their sheer abundance of quality. Two wooden rides are among the best of their type, and two of the steelies are also top ten material. All of the roller coasters at this park are of the thrill variety, even the park's runaway mine train, often the type of ride designed exclusively for the family trade. Those in search of kick-ass roller coasters will love this park.

6. BLACKPOOL PLEASURE BEACH

Blackpool, England

Four classic wooden roller coasters, along with one of the tallest steel rides in the world, are the major attractions at this ten-coaster park, a hundred-year-old British institution. Ironically, this is one of the few places left in the world where you can have a good old-fashioned *American* amusement park experience.

7. PARAMOUNT'S KINGS DOMINION

Doswell, Virginia

This wonderful park has the distinction of containing the most wooden roller coasters of any park in North America, a total of four (and ties England's Blackpool Pleasure Beach for the most in the world). Among the steel rides

〰〰〰〰〰〰〰〰〰〰〰〰〰〰〰〰〰〰〰〰〰〰〰〰〰〰〰〰〰〰

Roller Coaster Fact: Paramount's Kings Dominion, north of Richmond, Virginia, and Blackpool Pleasure Beach, Blackpool, England, tie for having the most wooden roller coasters—four each, although Blackpool also has a wooden-tracked Wild Mouse.

〰〰〰〰〰〰〰〰〰〰〰〰〰〰〰〰〰〰〰〰〰〰〰〰〰〰〰〰〰〰

offered, one is built almost entirely over water and, in fact, is the only roller coaster in the world that dives into an underwater tunnel. The other eight roller coasters at the park offer a wide and unique variety of thrills.

8. SIX FLAGS GREAT AMERICA

Gurnee, Illinois

The great variety is what sets this collection of rides apart from others. From stand-up to sit-down, giant wood to inverted, it's all represented in the eight scream machines here. One of them is a family-oriented device; the others are all-out thrill rides.

9. SIX FLAGS OVER TEXAS

Arlington, Texas

Like Six Flags Over Georgia, this grouping of coasters is of the more traditional kind, and of great quality. What sets it apart is that it offers several family-type rides. It also offers the Texas Giant, considered by many, including this author, to be the world's number one roller coaster.

10. KENNYWOOD

West Mifflin, Pennsylvania

This is "America's finest traditional park." It is also a National Historic Landmark. Five roller coasters are offered, but don't go to this park looking for the ultimate in thrills. Only one of the steel rides, Steel Phantom, will offer big thrills—huge, in fact, as it is the tallest looping-steel coaster in the world, and its 80-plus mph speed makes it the world's fastest roller coaster. Believe it or not, however, it's the three landmark wooden coasters that are the real attraction at Kennywood. Each began life in the 1920s, each has been meticulously maintained over the years, and each contains design elements typical of the Golden Age of roller coasters in which they were built. They're not of any great size, and they don't offer serious, heavy-duty thrills, but they make up for that by utilizing the undulating, hilly terrain they are built on to hide surprise after giddy surprise. Most important, they offer us the rare chance to experience something exactly the way folks did over seventy years ago. While other parks feverishly construct new wooden coasters that evoke those of the 1920s, Kennywood's cherished collection is the genuine article. It is a privilege to ride these time-honored works of art.

Also Worth Mentioning

• SIX FLAGS ASTROWORLD, Houston, Texas.   Nine roller coasters of every conceivable shape, size, intensity, and variety. The park's Ultra Twister is the only ride of its kind in the Western Hemisphere.

• BUSCH GARDENS, Williamsburg, Virginia.   Five coasters, including a classic steel looping, the world's first suspended, a giant inverted, and, of all things, a Wild Mouse (a compact steel coaster with a wildly zigzagging track) that is an absolute hoot.

• BUSCH GARDENS, Tampa, Florida.   Home to two of the best steel roller coasters on the planet, as well as two family-friendly looping steel coasters.

• SIX FLAGS GREAT ADVENTURE, Jackson, New Jersey.   Nine different roller coaster tracks (on seven different roller coasters) offer great variety for every family member. The park's Great American Scream Machine was the tallest roller coaster in the world when it opened in 1989.

• SIX FLAGS ST. LOUIS, Allenton, Missouri.   Five coasters, three of which could be considered among the best of their kind in the world.

• DORNEY PARK, Allentown, Pennsylvania.   Classic wood, modern wood, classic steel, huge steel, Dorney's no-nonsense collection offers something for everyone.

• HERSHEYPARK, Hershey, Pennsylvania.   Another no-nonsense collection of both wooden and looping steel roller coasters, several for the entire family, a few outright thrillers.

Roller Coaster Fact: The steepest drops on roller coasters have rarely been more than 60 degrees, until the 1997 debut of Batman and Robin—The Chiller at Six Flags Great Adventure (Jackson, New Jersey) and Mr. Freeze at both Six Flags Over Texas (Arlington, Texas) and Six Flags St. Louis (Allenton, Missouri). All three feature 90-degree drops from a height of well over 100 feet—that's straight down, folks!

8 THE GUIDE TO ROLLER COASTERS WORLDWIDE

The guide to roller coasters worldwide lists all operating wooden roller coasters and most steel. Each listing includes the name of the ride, whether it is made of wood or steel, the type of coaster it is, and a rating, plus any comments about the ride that may be of interest.

The two-part rating system is exclusive to *The Roller Coaster Lover's Companion.* The first rating, "Level of Intensity" (referred to in the guide as "Level"), measures the ride's physical intensity: that is, the amount of flipping, slamming, and bouncing; and the severity of the force of gravity that the passenger is subjected to. A Level 1 ride is the most gentle; Level 5 is the most severe. Use this rating to determine whether children, seniors, or coaster novices should attempt to climb aboard. The second rating is a "Star" rating, from one to five, referring to the ride quality. One star is the poorest; five stars, the best. A ride rated "Level 5 ★★," indicates a very physical experience, yet extremely lacking in quality. A "Level 5 ★★★★★ Super Screamer" is the wildest, most rambunctious ride, superior in design, operation, and maintenance.

These ratings are based on my own experiences riding the rides, as well as input from other coaster enthusiasts, casual fans, and published top ten lists. Unless otherwise noted, all parks listed operate seasonally, usually from spring to fall. Parks that are open early or late in the season tend to operate only on weekends and holidays during those periods. It is highly recommended that you call ahead for exact days and hours of operation.

Additionally, parks will be more than happy to provide guests with precise directions and information about accommodations in the area.

It is also recommended that you call the park to ensure that the roller coasters you desire to ride will be operational on the day of your visit. Regularly scheduled maintenance work, especially at parks that are open year-round, or a persistent mechanical problem may leave unknowing visitors extremely disappointed. Of course, unforeseen mechanical difficulties may require that a ride be shut down on the day of your visit; if that happens, the only solution is to grin and bear it. Rides that are unavailable are usually posted each day outside the park at the ticket booths. You may also check with Guest Services.

When traveling abroad, you might want to consult a knowledgeable travel agent for more insight regarding coasters in the area.

ASIA

CHINA

Ocean Park, Hong Kong
   1. DRAGON, Steel Looping; Level 3   ★★★

INDIA

Esselworld, New Delhi
   1. LITTLE DIPPER, Wood Out and Back; Level 2   ★★★

JAPAN

Many of the parks in this country operate year-round. Americans: Beware of the high costs to ride Japanese coasters due to the poor exchange rate.

Expoland, Osaka 06-877-0560
   1. LOOP CORKSCREW, Steel Looping; Level 3   ★★★
   2. OROCHI, Steel Inverted; Level 5   ★★★★★
     (This B&M creation is a mirror image of Cedar Point's Raptor.)
   3. WILD MOUSE, Compact Steel; Level 3   ★★★

Fantasy Dome, Tomakomai
   1. SUPER ROLLER COASTER, Steel Non-looping; Level 4   ★★★★

Fujikyu Highlands, Osaka 0555-24-6888
   1. FUJIYAMA, Steel Non-looping; Level 5   ★★★★★ Super Screamer
     (The world's tallest full-circuit roller coaster.)
   2. MOONSAULT SCRAMBLE, Steel Looping Shuttle; Level 5   ★★★★
   3. WILD MOUSE, Compact Steel; Level 3   ★★★★

Family Land, Gotemba
1. GAMBIT, Steel Inverted; Level 5   ★★★★★
   This B&M coaster is similar to Batman—The Ride, found at five Six
   Flags theme parks in the United States.
2. STAND-UP COASTER, Steel Looping Stand-up; Level 4   ★★★

Hakkeijima Sea Paradise, Yokohama
1. SURF COASTER, Steel Non-looping; Level 4   ★★★★
   (Part of this fascinating ride, extending into the Sea of Japan, is built
   on pontoons.)

Himeji Central Park, Himeji
1. DIAVIO, Steel Inverted; Level 5   ★★★★★

Kijima Resort, Kijima
1. JUPITER, Wood Twister; Level 4   ★★★★
   (Opened in 1993, after a lifting of restrictions regarding wooden structures of any significant height, this was the first wooden roller coaster
   ever to be built in Japan.)

Koraku-en Amusement Park, Tokyo 03-58-00-9999
This park redefines the term "urban amusement park." It is located right
in the heart of Japan's capital city.
1. ROLLER COASTER, Steel Non-looping; Level 3   ★★★

Mukogaoka Amusement Park, Mukogaoka
1. DIOS, Steel Non-looping; Level 4   ★★★★

Nagashima Spaland, Mei-ken 059-4-45-1111
1. CORKSCREW, Steel Looping; Level 2   ★★
2. LOOPING STAR, Steel Looping; Level 3   ★★★
3. WHITE CYCLONE, Wood Twister; Level 5   ★★★★★ Super Screamer
4. WILD MOUSE, Compact Steel; Level 3   ★★★

Nasu Highlands, Nasu
1. F:2, Steel Inverted; Level 5   ★★★★

Parque España, Osaka
1. PYRENEES, Steel Inverted; Level 5   ★★★★★

Portopia Land, Hyogo-Ken 078-302-2820
1. ANDALUSIAN RAILROAD, Steel; Level 3   ★★★
2. BAVARIAN MOUNTAIN RAILROAD, Steel Non-looping; Level 3   ★★★★
3. DOUBLE LOOP, Steel Looping; Level 3   ★★★★

Seibu-en Amusement Park, Seibu-en
1. Loop Screw, Steel Looping; Level 3 ★★★★

Space World, Kita-Kyushu-shi 09-36-72-3600
1. Titan, Steel Non-looping; Level 5 ★★★★

Summerland, Tokyo 0425-586511
1. Hayabusa, Steel Suspended; Level 4 ★★★★

Tokyo Disneyland, Tokyo 0473-54-0001
1. Big Thunder Mountain Railroad, Steel Mine Train; Level 3 ★★★
2. Gadget's Go Coaster, Compact Steel; Level 2 ★★★

Yomiuriland, Tokyo 81-449661111
1. Bandit, Steel Non-looping; Level 5 ★★★★★ Super Screamer
(This massive ride starts out with a lift height of 167 feet, eventually plunging into a gully, which provides this monster with a vertical spread of 256 feet.)
2. White Canyon, Wood Twister; Level 3 ★★★★
(Designed, engineered, and prefabricated entirely in the United States, this is only the third wooden roller coaster ever built in Japan. It is patterned after the original Coney Island Cyclone and, in fact, is the largest copy of that legend built to date.)

KOREA

Everland, Seoul
1. Fortress of Eagle, Steel Suspended; Level 4 ★★★★

AUSTRALIA

Australia's Wonderland, Sydney
The two wooden coasters in this park are patterned after the junior woodies and the rides known as Grizzly at the North American Paramount parks.
1. Beastie, Wood Junior; Level 2 ★★★
2. Bush Beast, Wood Twister; Level 3 ★★★
3. Vampire, Steel Looping Shuttle; Level 4 ★★★

Dreamworld, Coomera 61-7-5588-1111
1. Thunderbolt, Steel Looping; Level 4 ★★★★
2. Tower of Terror, Steel Non-looping Shuttle; Level 5 ★★★
(This ride is a single-track version of the 100 mph, 400-foot-tall Superman—The Escape at Six Flags Magic Mountain, in California.)

Luna Park, Melbourne
1. SCENIC RAILWAY, Wood Out and Back; Level 3   ★★★

Warner Bros. Movie World, Brisbane 07-5573-8485
1. LETHAL WEAPON—THE RIDE, Steel Inverted Level 5   ★★★★

NEW ZEALAND

Rainbow's End Amusement Park, Christchurch
1. CORKSCREW, Steel Looping; Level 3   ★★

EUROPE

AUSTRIA

Prater Park, Vienna
1. HOCHBAHN, Compact Steel; Level 3   ★★★
2. LOOPING BAHN, Compact Steel Looping; Level 3   ★★★

BELGIUM

Bobbejaanland, Kasterlee 3214-557-811
1. AIR RACE, Steel Suspended; Level 2   ★★★
2. LOOPING STAR, Steel Looping; Level 3   ★★★
3. REVOLUTION, Enclosed Steel Non-looping; Level 2   ★★
4. TORNADO, Steel Looping; Level 3   ★★

Walibi, Wavre 3210-414466
1. COLORADO, Steel Mine Train; Level 3   ★★★
2. SIROCCO, Steel Looping Shuttle; Level: 3   ★★★★
3. TORNADO, Compact Steel Non-looping; Level 3   ★★★

DENMARK

Bakken, Klampenborg
1. RUTSCHEBANEN, Wood Twister; Level 3   ★★★★

Tivoli Gardens, Copenhagen 45-33-151001
1. RUTSCHEBANEN, Wood Twister; Level 3   ★★★★

FINLAND

Linnanmaki Park, Helsinki 358-077-3991
1. VUORISTORATA, Wood Twister; Level 4   ★★★★

FRANCE

Disneyland Paris, Cedex 33-164-743000
1. BIG THUNDER MOUNTAIN RAILROAD, Steel Mine Train;
   Level 3 ★★★★
2. GADGET'S GO COASTER, Steel Junior; Level 2 ★★★
3. LE TEMPLE DE PÉRIL, Steel Looping; Level 3 ★★★
4. SPACE MOUNTAIN, Enclosed Steel Looping; Level 4 ★★★★

Parc Astérix, Plailly 33-44-623131
1. GOUDURIX, Steel Looping; Level 4 ★★★★
2. LE TRAN'S ARVERNE, Steel; Level 2 ★★★
3. TONERRE DE ZEUS, Wood Twister; Level 4 ★★★★★

Walibi Stroumpf, Metz 33-87-519052
1. ANACONDA, Wood Out and Back; Level 4 ★★★★
2. SPACE COMET, Steel Looping; Level 3 ★★★

GERMANY

Europa Park, Rust 49-7822-770
1. EURO MIR, Steel Non-looping; Level 3 ★★★★
2. GROTTEN BLITZ, Enclosed Steel Non-looping; Level 2 ★★★

Hansa Park, Neustadt-Holstein 49-4563-7088
1. NESSIE, Steel Looping; Level 3 ★★★

Heide Park, Soltau 49-5191-5022
1. BIG LOOP, Steel Looping; Level 3 ★★★
2. BOBBAHN 1, Steel Non-looping; Level 2 ★★★
3. BOBBAHN 2, Steel Non-looping; Level 2 ★★★

Phantasialand, Bruhl 49-2232-36242
1. COLORADO ADVENTURE, Steel Mine Train; Level 3 ★★★
2. GEBIRGSBAHN, Steel Non-looping; Level 3 ★★★
3. SPACE CENTER, Steel Non-looping; Level 4 ★★★★

Warner Bros. Movie World, Bottrop, Kirchhellen 49-2045-8990
1. LETHAL WEAPON—THE RIDE, Enclosed Steel Looping;
   Level 4 ★★★★

GREAT BRITAIN

England

Alton Towers, Staffordshire 01538-702200
Height restrictions require that no ride in this beautiful park rise above the treetops. To meet this demand, the clever folks who run the park dug pits to place their roller coasters in!
1. BLACK HOLE, Enclosed Compact Steel; Level 3 ★★★
2. CORKSCREW, Steel Looping; Level 3 ★★★
3. MINI APPLE, Steel Kiddie; Level 1 ★★
4. NEMESIS, Steel Inverted; Level 4 ★★★★
   (One of the most heavily themed roller coasters in the world, this ride constantly dives into pits and tunnels dug into the ground.)
5. THUNDER LOOPER, Steel Looping Shuttle; Level 4 ★★★★

Blackpool Pleasure Beach, Blackpool 01253-341033
This is Europe's premier amusement park, with literally dozens of rides packed into a scant forty acres. It is not uncommon for rides to be built over, under, and through other rides, and the park contains many old-time classic rides that no longer exist anywhere else in the world. Oddly enough, although located in Great Britain, the park is the epitome of an old-fashioned American amusement park.
1. AVALANCHE, Steel Bobsled; Level 4 ★★★★
2. BIG DIPPER, Wood Out and Back; Level 4 ★★★★
3. CIRCUS CLOWN, Steel Kiddie; Level 1 ★★
4. GRAND NATIONAL, Wood Dual-track Out and Back; Level 4 ★★★★
5. PEPSI MAX BIG ONE, Steel Non-looping; Level 3 ★★★
6. REVOLUTION, Steel Looping Shuttle; Level 3 ★★
7. ROLLER COASTER, Wood Out and Back; Level 3 ★★★
8. SPACE INVADERS, Enclosed Compact Steel; Level 3 ★★★★
9. STEEPLECHASE, Steel Triple-track; Level 3 ★★★★
   (Those familiar with the old Coney Island, New York ride of the same name will be thrilled to know that a modern version of the ride exists here at Blackpool. Passengers ride on horses that race along an undulating course, just like that famous original. This is the only existing ride of its kind in the world.)
10. WILD MOUSE, Compact Wood Twister; Level 5 ★★★★
    (This is one of the original wooden Wild Mouse rides from the 1950s, the likes of which do not exist in the United States any longer.)
11. ZIPPER DIPPER, Wood Junior Out and Back; Level 2 ★★★

~~~~~~

Roller Coaster Fact: The Kennywood Racer, La Fería's Serpiente de Fuego, and Blackpool's Grand National only appear to be dual-track racing coasters. All three are actually continuous single-track coasters, which is why trains leaving the station on one side will return to the other side at ride's end.

~~~~~~

Camelot, Lancashire 01257-453044
1. TOWER OF TERROR, Enclosed Steel Looping; Level 4 ★★★★

Chessington World of Adventures, Surrey 01372-727227
1. CLOWN AROUND, Steel Kiddie; Level 1 ★★
2. VAMPIRE, Steel Suspended; Level 3 ★★★

Drayton Manor, Staffordshire 01827-287979
1. KLONDIKE GOLD MINE, Compact Steel Looping; Level 3 ★★★
2. MINI DRAGON, Steel Kiddie; Level 1 ★★★
3. 7-UP SHOCKWAVE, Steel Looping Stand-up; Level 4 ★★★★

Dreamland Fun Park, Margate, Kent 01843-227011
1. BIG APPLE, Steel Kiddie; Level 1 ★★
2. LADYBIRD, Steel Non-looping; Level 1 ★★
3. SCENIC RAILWAY, Wood Out and Back; Level 3 ★★★

Flamingo Land, North Yorkshire 01653-668-287
1. BULLET, Steel Looping Shuttle; Level 5 ★★★★
2. CORKSCREW, Steel Looping; Level 3 ★★★
3. DRAGON, Steel Non-looping; Level 1 ★★
4. FLYING TRAPEZE, Compact Steel Non-looping; Level 2 ★★★
5. THUNDER MOUNTAIN, Enclosed Steel; Level 2 ★★★

Frontier Land, Morcambe 01524-410024
1. AMERICAN COASTER, Steel Kiddie; Level 1 ★★
2. BUFFALO STAMPEDE, Compact Steel Non-looping; Level 2 ★★
3. RATTLER, Steel Kiddie; Level 1 ★★
4. RUNAWAY MINE TRAIN, Compact Wood Twister; Level 4 ★★★★
   (One of the few wooden wild mouse rides left in all the world.)
5. STAMPEDE, Steel Non-looping; Level 3 ★★★
6. TEXAS TORNADO, Wood Out and Back; Level 3 ★★★
   (One car on this coaster's train faces backward.)

Great Yarmouth Pleasure Beach, Norfolk 01493-844585
1. LOOPING STAR, Steel Looping; LEVEL 3   ★★★
2. ROLLER COASTER, Wood Twister; Level 3   ★★★

Gulliver's World, Warrington 01925-444888
1. ANTELOPE, Wood Twister; Level 3   ★★★

Lightwater Valley, North Yorkshire 01765-635321
1. RAT, Enclosed Compact Steel; Level 3   ★★★★
(Riders must climb through a sewer-pipe opening and walk through a tight, dark tunnel before boarding this coaster, which is constructed completely underground, in the dark.)
2. ULTIMATE, Steel Terrain; Level 4   ★★★★
(This is the world's longest roller coaster. With two lift hills during its 7,542 feet of track, it also provides the longest roller coaster ride time: a staggering six minutes!)

Southport Pleasure Beach, Southport
1. BIG APPLE, Steel Kiddie; Level 1   ★★
2. CYCLONE, Wood Twister; Level 3   ★★★
(One car on this ride's train faces backward.)
3. WILDCAT, Compact Steel Non-looping; Level 2   ★★

Thorpe Park, Surrey 01932-565298
1. X:/NO WAY OUT, Enclosed Steel; Level 3   ★★★

Wales

Oakwood Leisure Park, Pembrokeshire 01834-891373
1. MEGAFOBIA, Wood Twister; Level 5   ★★★★★ Super Screamer
(The largest wooden coaster in Great Britain.)

HUNGARY

Vidam Park, Budapest
1. HULLAMVISIT, Wood Twister; Level 2   ★★★

ITALY

Mirabilandia, Ravenna
1. HURRICANE, Compact Steel; Level 2   ★★
2. SIERRA TONANTE, Wood Twister; Level 4   ★★★★

THE NETHERLANDS

De Eftelling, Kaatsheuvel 0-416-788-111
1. PEGASUS, Wood Twister; Level 2   ★★★
2. PYTHON, Steel Looping; Level 2   ★★★

Walibi Flavo, Dronten 031-321-11514
1. EL CONDOR, Steel Inverted; Level 5   ★★★

SPAIN

Port Aventura, Tarragona 34-77779033
1. DRAGON KHAN, Steel Looping; Level 5   ★★★★★ Super Screamer
   (This magnificent creation holds the current world record for spinning its riders upside down: eight, count 'em, eight breathtaking times!)
2. EL DIABLO, Steel Mine Train; Level 2   ★★
3. STAMPIDA, Wood Dual-track Twister; Level 4   ★★★★★
   (The first giant wooden racing coaster built in twelve years, and a real thriller.)
4. TOMAHAWK, Wood Junior Out and Back; Level 2   ★★★
   (This family coaster actually snuggles beside the larger Stampida and cuts through its bigger brother's structure, almost providing park guests with a triple-racing coaster.)

SWEDEN

Grona Lund Amusement Park, Stockholm
1. JETLINE, Steel Non-looping; Level 4   ★★★★

Liseberg, Gothenburg 460-31-400-100
1. HANGOVER, Steel Inverted Shuttle; Level 4   ★★★★
2. LISEBERGBANEN, Steel Non-looping Terrain; Level 4   ★★★★

NORTH AMERICA
CANADA

Alberta

Calaway Park, Calgary, Alberta (403) 240-3822
1. TURN OF THE CENTURY, Steel Looping; Level 3   ★★★

Galaxyland, Edmonton, Alberta (403) 444-5300
A fully enclosed amusement park, in the heart of the world's largest combination shopping mall and entertainment center.
1. AUTO SLED, Steel Non-looping; Level 2 ★★★
2. MINDBENDER, Steel Looping; Level 5 ★★★★
   (A three-looping coaster by Anton Schwarzkopf that features some of the strongest positive g-forces on any roller coaster in North America.)

British Columbia

Playland Amusement Park, Vancouver, British Columbia (604) 255-5161
This seasonal amusement park operates as the midway for the Pacific National Exhibition for several weeks in late summer.
1. CORKSCREW, Steel Looping; Level 3 ★★★
2. ROLLER COASTER, Wood Twister; Level 4 ★★★★
3. SUPER BIG GULP, Compact Steel; Level 3 ★★★

New Brunswick

Crystal Palace, Dieppe, New Brunswick
Located indoors in a shopping mall, the park is open year-round.
1. CRYSTAL BULLET, Steel Junior; Level 2 ★★★

Nova Scotia

Upper Clements Family Theme Park, Clementsport, Nova Scotia (902) 532-7557
1. TREE TOPPER, Wood Out and Back; Level 3 ★★★

Ontario

Chippewa Park, Thunder Bay, Ontario (807) 622-9777
1. ROLLER COASTER, Steel Junior; Level 2 ★★

Marineland, Niagara Falls, Ontario (416) 356-8250
1. DRAGON MOUNTAIN, Steel Looping; Level 3 ★★★★
2. TIVOLI, Steel Kiddie; Level 1 ★★★

Paramount Canada's Wonderland, Vaughan, Ontario (416) 832-7000
Part of the Paramount Parks theme park chain, containing the biggest collection of roller coasters in Canada. The park's two wooden roller coasters were patterned after two classic rides that once existed at Ohio's old Coney Island in Cincinnati.

1. BAT, Steel Looping Shuttle; Level 4   ★★★
2. DRAGON FYRE, Steel Looping; Level 3   ★★★
3. GHOSTER COASTER, Wood Junior; Level 2   ★★★
4. MIGHTY CANADIAN MINEBUSTER, Wood Out and Back; Level 4   ★★★★
5. SKYRIDER, Steel Stand-up; Level 4   ★★★
6. TOP GUN, Steel Inverted; Level 5   ★★★★
7. VORTEX, Steel Suspended; Level 4   ★★★★
8. WILDE BEAST, Wood Twister; Level 4   ★★★★

Quebec

La Ronde Amusement Park, Montreal, Quebec (514) 872-6120
Located on an island in the St. Lawrence River that is also home to a water park and an aquarium.
1. COBRA, Steel Stand-up; Level 4   ★★★★
2. LE BOOMERANG, Steel Looping Shuttle; Level 4   ★★★
3. LE DRAGON, Enclosed Steel Junior; Level 3   ★★★
4. LE MONSTRE, Wood Dual-track Twister; Level 4   ★★★★
5. LE SUPER MÉNAGE, Steel Looping; Level 3   ★★★
6. LES PETITES MONTAGNES RUSSES, Steel Kiddie; Level 1   ★★★

Les Galleries Capitale, Quebec City, Quebec (418) 627-5800
Part of an indoor shopping complex, the park is open year-round.
1. CAPITAL EXPRESS, Steel Junior; Level 2   ★★★

MEXICO

La Fería, Mexico City, Mexico 52-5/515-2945
1. CASCABEL, Steel Looping Shuttle; Level 4   ★★★★
2. SERPIENTE DE FUEGO, Wood Dual-track Out and Back; Level 4   ★★★★
3. TORNADO, Compact Steel; Level 3   ★★★

Reino Adventura, Mexico City, Mexico 52-5/652-1735
This park has the distinction of being the former home of the whale that starred in the *Free Willy* motion pictures. Odds are he never rode one of the park's coasters!
1. CATARINA VOLADORA, Steel Junior; Level 1   ★★★
2. ESCORPION, Steel Looping Shuttle; Level 4   ★★★
3. ROLLER SKATER, Steel Junior; Level 2   ★★★

UNITED STATES

Alabama

Waterville, USA, Gulf Shores, Alabama (205) 948-2106
This is a water park that expanded by adding go-kart tracks and a roller coaster. The non-water attractions are open year-round.
1. CANNONBALL, Wood Out and Back; Level 3   ★★★★

Arizona

Castles and Coasters, Phoenix, Arizona (602) 997-7576
1. DESERT STORM, Steel Looping; Level 3   ★★
2. PATRIOT, Steel Junior; Level 1   ★★★

California

Belmont Park, San Diego, California (619) 488-1549
Belmont Park was at one time a full-fledged seaside amusement park. It closed in the 1970s, leaving only the classic wooden roller coaster standing. Local preservation efforts rebuilt the coaster, and it now operates as a stand-alone attraction, together with a carousel, as part of a shopping center. Attractions at this park are open daily, year-round.
1. GIANT DIPPER, Wood Twister; Level 4   ★★★★

Disneyland, Anaheim, California (714) 999-4000
The granddaddy of all theme parks, currently under expansion. When finished, it will include an entirely new, second theme park on the site of the current parking lot. The park is open daily, year-round.
1. BIG THUNDER MOUNTAIN RAILROAD, Mine Train; Level 2   ★★★★
2. GADGET'S GO COASTER, Steel Junior; Level 1   ★★★
3. MATTERHORN BOBSLED, Dual-track Steel Non-looping;
   Level 2   ★★★★
4. SPACE MOUNTAIN, Enclosed Steel Non-looping; Level 3   ★★★★

Knott's Berry Farm, Buena Park, California (714) 827-1776
The park is open daily, year-round.
1. BOOMERANG, Steel Looping Shuttle; Level 4   ★★★
2. JAGUAR, Steel Non-looping; Level 2   ★★★
3. MONTEZOOMA'S REVENGE, Steel Looping Shuttle; Level 4   ★★★★
4. TIMBERLINE TWISTER, Steel Kiddie; Level 1   ★★★
5. WINDJAMMER, Steel Looping; Level 4   ★★★

Pacific Pier, Santa Monica, California
This is the famous Santa Monica Pier, recently refurbished, with added attractions including a full amusement park.
1. WEST COASTER, Steel Non-looping; Level 2   ★★

Paramount's Great America, Santa Clara, California (408) 988-1800
Opened in 1976 by the Marriott Hotel Corporation, the park changed hands several times before being purchased by Paramount, primarily known for its motion picture productions.
1. DEMON, Steel Looping; Level 3   ★★★
2. GREEN SLIME MINE CAR COASTER, Steel Junior; Level 1   ★★★
3. GRIZZLY, Wood Twister; Level 3   ★★★
4. TIDAL WAVE, Steel Looping Shuttle; Level 4   ★★★★
5. TOP GUN, Steel Inverted; Level 4   ★★★★
6. VORTEX, Steel Stand-up; Level 4   ★★★★

Santa Cruz Beach Boardwalk, Santa Cruz, California (408) 423-5590
The last remaining oceanside boardwalk amusement park on the West Coast. The entire park is a National Historic Landmark. Open weekends year-round, daily spring through fall.
1. GIANT DIPPER, Wood Twister; Level 4   ★★★★
2. HURRICANE, Steel Non-looping; Level 3   ★★★★

Scandia Family Fun Center, Ontario, California (909) 390-3092
1. SCANDIA SCREAMER, Steel Non-looping; Level 3   ★★★

Six Flags Magic Mountain, Valencia, California (818) 992-0884
Open weekends year-round, daily spring through fall.
1. BATMAN—THE RIDE, Steel Inverted; Level 5   ★★★★★ Super Screamer
2. COLOSSUS, Wood Dual-track Out and Back; Level 4   ★★★★
3. FLASHBACK, Steel Non-looping; Level 5   ★★
4. GOLD RUSHER, Mine Train; Level 2   ★★★
5. NINJA, Steel Suspended; Level 4   ★★★★
6. PSYCLONE, Wood Twister Level 4   ★★★★
   (The design for this coaster is based on the original Coney Island Cyclone in Brooklyn, New York.)
7. REVOLUTION, Steel Looping; Level 4   ★★★★
   (This was the first roller coaster built in modern times to feature a 360-degree vertical loop.)

Santa Cruz's Giant Dipper is a National Historic Landmark. (Courtesy of Dennis McNulty)

   8. SPEEDY GONZALEZ, Steel Kiddie; Level 1 ★★★
   9. SUPERMAN—THE ESCAPE, Steel Non-looping Shuttle; Level 5 ★★★★
      (Currently the world's tallest and fastest thrill ride. Its height of 415
      feet and top speed of 100 mph should keep it in that spot for a *long*
      time to come.)
   10. VIPER, Steel Looping; Level 5 ★★★★

Colorado

   Elitch Gardens, Denver, Colorado (303) 455-4771
      1. MIND ERASER, Steel Inverted; Level 5 ★★★★
      2. SIDEWINDER, Steel Looping Shuttle; Level 3 ★★
      3. TWISTER II, Wood Twister; Level 4 ★★★★

   Lakeside Amusement Park, Denver, Colorado (303) 477-1621
      1. CYCLONE, Wood Twister; Level 3 ★★★★
      2. WILD CHIPMUNK, Compact Steel Non-looping; Level 4 ★★★★

The Lakeside Cyclone, Denver, circling over its art-deco style station. (Courtesy of Bobby Nagy)

Connecticut

Lake Compounce, Bristol, Connecticut (860)583-3631

The oldest continuously operating amusement park in the country, it got a major face lift for the 1997 season, ensuring that it will be around for many generations to come.

1. ZOOMERANG, Steel Looping Shuttle; Level 4   ★★★
2. WILDCAT, Wood Twister; Level 3   ★★★★

Quassy Amusement Park, Middlebury, CT (203) 758-2913

1. MONSTER MOUSE, Compact Steel Non-looping; Level 2   ★★
2. KIDDIE COASTER, Steel Kiddie; Level 1   ★

Florida

Busch Gardens, Tampa, Florida (813) 987-5000

The combination of Kumba and Montu provides this park with an unbeatable pair—these are two of the best steel roller coasters currently operating. Open daily, year-round.

1. KUMBA, Steel Looping; Level 5   ★★★★★ Super Screamer
2. MONTU, Steel Inverted; Level 5   ★★★★★ Super Screamer
3. PYTHON, Steel Looping; Level 3   ★★
4. SCORPION, Steel Looping; Level 3   ★★★

The Magic Kingdom at Walt Disney World, Lake Buena Vista, Florida (407) 828-2100

Open daily, year-round.

1. THE BARNSTORMER, Steel Junior; Level 1   ★★★
2. BIG THUNDER MOUNTAIN RAILROAD, Mine Train; Level 2   ★★★★
3. SPACE MOUNTAIN, Enclosed Steel Non-looping; Level 2   ★★★

Kumba roars through
Busch Gardens,
Tampa. (Courtesy of
Bobby Nagy)

Miracle Strip Amusement Park, Panama City, Florida (904) 234-3333
1. STARLINER, Wood Out and Back; Level 3   ★★★★

Old Town, Kissimmee, Florida
1. WINDSTORM, Compact Steel; Level 3   ★★★

Georgia

Lake Winnepesaukah, Rossville, Georgia (770) 866-5681
1. CANNON BALL, Wood Out and Back; Level 3   ★★★★
2. WACKY WORM, Steel Kiddie; Level 1   ★★

Six Flags Over Georgia, Atlanta, Georgia (770) 948-9290
This was the second park that the Six Flags Company built. Without a doubt, it is also their best.

1. BATMAN—THE RIDE, Steel Inverted; Level 5   ★★★★★ Super Screamer
2. DAHLONEGA MINE TRAIN, Mine Train; Level 2   ★★★
3. GEORGIA CYCLONE, Wood Twister; Level 5   ★★★★★ Super Screamer
4. GREAT AMERICAN SCREAM MACHINE, Wood Out and Back; Level 4   ★★★★
5. MIND BENDER, Steel Looping; Level 5   ★★★★★ Super Screamer
6. NINJA, Steel Looping; Level 5   ★★★★
7. VIPER, Steel Looping Shuttle; Level 4   ★★★★

Idaho

Silverwood Theme Park, Athol, Idaho (208) 772-0515
1. GRAVITY DEFYING CORKSCREW, Steel Looping; Level 2   ★★
   (Originally located at Knott's Berry Farm in California, this was the very first coaster built in modern times that went upside down, and it led the way to the construction of the giant looping monsters we enjoy today at so many parks.)
2. GRIZZLY, Wood Out and Back; Level 3   ★★★★

Illinois

Hillcrest Park, Lake Zurich, Illinois (708) 438-0140
Park open only for private picnic events.
1. LITTLE DIPPER, Wood Junior; Level 1   ★★★

Kiddieland, Melrose Park, Illinois (708) 343-8003
1. LITTLE DIPPER, Wood Junior; Level 1   ★★★

Six Flags Great America, Gurnee, Illinois (708) 249-1776
1. AMERICAN EAGLE, Wood Dual-track Out and Back; Level 4   ★★★★
   (With a drop of 147 feet, this is the world's tallest dual-track racing roller coaster.)
2. BATMAN—THE RIDE, Steel Inverted; Level 5   ★★★★★ Super Screamer
   (The world's first below-the-track, chair-lift-style, legs-dangling roller coaster.)
3. DEMON, Steel Looping; Level 3   ★★★
4. IRON WOLF, Steel Stand-up; Level 5   ★★★★
5. SHOCK WAVE, Steel Looping; Level 5   ★★★★

6. VIPER, Wood Twister; Level 4   ★★★★
(Inspired by the Coney Island Cyclone, with a few interesting modifications.)
7. WHIZZER, Steel Non-looping; Level 2   ★★★★

Indiana

Fun Spot, Angola, Indiana (219) 833-2972
1. AFTERBURNER, Steel Looping Shuttle; Level 3   ★★

Holiday World, Santa Claus, Indiana (812) 937-4401
1. FIRECRACKER, Compact Steel; Level 2   ★★
2. RAVEN, Wood Terrain; Level 4   ★★★★★
(This park may be the epitome of a family entertainment place, so the addition of this ride was quite a surprise indeed, as it is one serious thrill ride. The Raven is responsible for redefining the limits to which a family thriller can reach.)

Indiana Beach, Monticello, Indiana (219) 583-4141
This is a complete resort, featuring all types of water sports, nightclubs, and restaurants in addition to the amusement park. A full hotel and private rental cabins are located within the park.
1. GALAXIE, Compact Steel; Level 2   ★★
2. HOOSIER HURRICANE, Wood Out and Back; Level 3   ★★★★
3. TIG'RR, Compact Steel; Level 3   ★★★

Iowa

Adventureland, Des Moines, Iowa (515) 266-2121
1. DRAGON, Steel Looping; Level 4   ★★
2. OUTLAW, Wood Twister; Level 3   ★★★★
3. TORNADO, Wood Out and Back; Level 3   ★★★★
4. UNDERGROUND, Wood Gravity Dark Ride; Level 1   ★★★★
(This ride is a modern reincarnation of the "scenic railways" that existed nearly a century ago.)
5. WILD RIDER, Compact Steel; Level 2   ★★

Arnolds Park, Arnolds Park, Iowa (712) 332-7781
1. GIANT COASTER, Wood Out and Back; Level 3   ★★★
2. LITTLE COASTER, Steel Kiddie; Level 1   ★

Kansas

Joyland Amusement Park, Wichita, Kansas (316) 684-0179
1. ROLLER COASTER, Wood Out and Back; Level 3   ★★★

Kentucky

Kentucky Kingdom, Louisville, Kentucky (502) 366-2231
1. CHANG, Steel Stand-up; Level 5 ★★★★ Super Screamer
   (Currently the world's longest, tallest and fastest stand-up coaster.)
2. ROLLER SKATER, Steel Junior; Level 1 ★★★
3. T^2 (Terror to the Second Power), Steel Inverted; Level 5 ★★★★
4. THUNDER RUN, Wood Twister; Level 4 ★★★★
5. VAMPIRE, Steel Looping Shuttle; Level 4 ★★★

Louisiana

City Park, New Orleans, Louisiana (504) 482-4888
1. LIVE OAK LADYBUG, Steel Junior; Level 1 ★★

Maryland

Adventure World, Largo, Maryland (301) 249-1500
1. CANNONBALL, Steel Kiddie; Level 1 ★★
2. MIND ERASER, Steel Inverted; Level 5 ★★★★
3. PYTHON, Steel Looping Shuttle; Level 3 ★★
4. WILD ONE, Wood Out and Back; Level 5 ★★★★
   (Originally located at Paragon Park near Boston, Massachusetts, the
   Wild One was one of the first wooden coasters to be completely relocated and rebuilt at another park.)

Trimper's Rides, Ocean City, Maryland (301) 289-8617
1. KIDDIE COASTER, Steel Kiddie; Level 1 ★★
2. TIDAL WAVE, Steel Looping Shuttle; Level 4 ★★★

Massachusetts

Riverside Park, Agawam, Massachusetts (413) 786-9300
1. BLACK WIDOW, Steel Looping Shuttle; Level 3 ★★
2. MIND ERASER, Steel Inverted; Level 5 ★★★★
3. RIVERSIDE CYCLONE, Wood Twister; Level 5 ★★★★★ Super
   Screamer
4. THUNDERBOLT, Wood Twister; Level 3 ★★★★

Roller Coaster Fact: Riverside Park's Thunderbolt (Agawam, Massachusetts) was based on plans from the Cyclone, a wooden roller coaster that operated at the Flushing, New York, World's Fair in 1939.

Whalom Park, Lunenburg, Massachusetts (508) 342-3707
1. FLYER COMET, Wood Twister; Level 3 ★★★★

Michigan

Michigan's Adventure, Muskegon, Michigan (616) 766-3377
1. CORKSCREW, Steel Looping; Level 3 ★★
2. WOLVERINE WILDCAT, Wood Twister; Level 3 ★★★★
3. ZACH'S ZOOMER, Wood Junior; Level 2 ★★★

Minnesota

Knott's Camp Snoopy, Bloomington, Minnesota (612) 883-8600
Mall of America, the largest shopping center in the United States, is the home of this indoor amusement park. Because of its indoor location, the park is open year round.
1. RIPSAW, Steel Non-looping; Level 1 ★★★

Valleyfair! Family Amusement Park, Shakopee, Minnesota (612) 445-7600
1. CORKSCREW, Steel Looping; Level 3 ★★★
2. EXCALIBUR, Steel Non-looping; Level 3 ★★★
    (Although this ride features a traditional wooden structure, its track is entirely comprised of the same kind of tubular steel used in all other steel coasters.
3. HIGH ROLLER, Wood Out and Back; Level 3 ★★★
4. MILD THING, Steel Kiddie; Level 1 ★★
5. WILD RAILS, Compact Steel; Level 2 ★★★
6. WILD THING, Steel Non-looping; Level 4 ★★★★
    (One of only seven full-circuit roller coasters in the world that reach a height of over 200 feet.)

Missouri

Silver Dollar City, Branson, Missouri (417) 338-2611
1. FIRE IN THE HOLE, Steel Gravity Dark Ride; Level 3 ★★★★
2. THUNDERATION, Mine Train; Level 4 ★★★★
    (Several cars on this thrilling mine train face backward.)

Six Flags St. Louis, Allenton, Missouri (314) 938-5300
1. ACME GRAVITY POWERED RAILROAD, Steel Kiddie; Level 1 ★★
2. BATMAN—THE RIDE, Steel Inverted; Level 5 ★★★★★ Super Screamer

3. Mr. Freeze, Steel Looping Shuttle; Level 4 ★★★★
4. Ninja, Steel Looping; Level 4 ★★★
5. River King Mine Ride, Mine Train; Level 2 ★★★★
6. Screamin' Eagle, Wood Out and Back; Level 4 ★★★★★ Super Screamer

Worlds of Fun, Kansas City, Missouri (816) 454-4545
1. Orient Express, Steel Looping; Level 4 ★★★★
2. Timber Wolf, Wood Twister; Level 4 ★★★★
3. Wacky Worm, Steel Kiddie; Level 1 ★★★
4. Zambezi Zinger, Steel Non-looping; Level 2 ★★★★

Mr. Freeze, Six Flags St. Louis, in its final stages of construction. (Courtesy of Six Flags St. Louis)

Nevada

All parks and attractions listed are part of large casino-resort hotels.

Buffalo Bill's Resort and Casino, Stateline, Nevada (702) 382-1212
1. DESPERADO, Steel Non-Looping; Level 5   ★★★★

Grand Slam Canyon, Las Vegas, Nevada (702) 794-3939
1. CANYON BLASTER, Steel Looping; Level 3   ★★★

MGM Grand Adventures, Las Vegas, Nevada (702) 739-1500
1. THUNDERBOLT, Steel Non-looping; Level 3   ★★★

New York New York Hotel and Casino, Las Vegas, Nevada (702) 740-6969
1. MANHATTAN EXPRESS, Steel Looping; Level 5   ★★★★
(The cars on this 203-foot-high coaster are themed to resemble New York City Yellow Taxi Cabs.)

Stratosphere Tower, Las Vegas, Nevada (702) 382-4446
1. HIGH ROLLER, Steel Junior; Level 3   ★★★
(Technically the world's "highest" roller coaster, due to its location at the top of a tower that is over 900 feet tall.)

New Hampshire

Canobie Lake Park, Salem, New Hampshire (603) 893-3506
1. CANOBIE CORKSCREW, Steel Looping; Level 3   ★★
2. GALAXIE, Compact Steel; Level 2   ★★★
3. YANKEE CANNONBALL, Wood Out and Back; Level 3   ★★★★

Santa's Village, Jefferson, New Hampshire (601) 586-4445
1. SANTA'S RAPID TRANSIT, Steel Junior; Level 2   ★★★

Story Land, Glen, New Hampshire (603) 383-4293
1. POLAR COASTER, Steel Junior; Level 2   ★★★

New Jersey

Casino Pier, Seaside Heights, New Jersey (908) 793-6488
1. JET STAR, Compact Steel; Level 3   ★★★
2. WIZARD'S CAVERN, Compact Enclosed Steel; Level 3   ★★★
(This unusual ride was first located at New Jersey's world-famous Palisades Amusement Park and was known as the Love Bugs.)

Clementon Lake Park, Clementon, New Jersey (609) 783-0263
1. JACK RABBIT, Wood Twister; Level 3   ★★★
   (This is the world's oldest operating wooden roller coaster, thrilling riders since 1919.)

Dinosaur Beach, Wildwood, New Jersey (609) 523-1440
1. CRAZY MOUSE, Compact Steel; Level 2   ★★★★
2. GOLDEN NUGGET MINE RIDE, Steel Gravity Dark Ride;
   Level 2   ★★★★

Funtown Pier, Seaside Park, New Jersey
1. ROLLER COAST LOOP, Compact Steel Looping; Level 3   ★★

Jenkinsons Pavilion, Point Pleasant, New Jersey (908) 899-0569
1. FLITZER, Compact Steel; Level 1   ★★

Keansburg Amusement Park, Keansburg, New Jersey (908) 495-5207
1. LITTLE DIPPER, Steel Kiddie; Level 1   ★★
2. SCREAMIN' DEMON, Compact Steel; Level 2   ★★★

Morey's Piers, The Wildwoods, New Jersey (609) 729-3700
The three separate piers that comprise Morey's Piers contain over seventy rides, the most of any amusement place in the world.

Mariner's Landing
1. GALAXIE, Compact Steel; Level 2   ★★
2. SEA SERPENT, Steel Looping Shuttle; Level 3   ★★★

Morey's Pier
1. FLITZER, Compact Steel; Level 1   ★★
2. GREAT NOR'EASTER, Steel Inverted; Level 5   ★★★★
3. JET STAR, Compact Steel; Level 2   ★★★

Wild Wheels Pier
1. GREAT WHITE, Wood Twister; Level 5   ★★★★★ Super Screamer

Nickel's Midway Pier, Wildwood, New Jersey (609) 522-2542
1. PYTHON, Compact Steel; Level 2   ★★

Playland, Ocean City, New Jersey
1. FLITZER, Compact Steel; Level 1   ★★
2. PYTHON, Compact Steel Looping; Level 3   ★★★
3. WILD MOUSE, Compact Steel; Level 2   ★★★

Six Flags Great Adventure, Jackson, New Jersey (908) 928-2000
This is the largest seasonal theme park in the country.
1. BATMAN AND ROBIN—THE CHILLER, Steel Dual-track Shuttle; Level 5   ★★★★
2. BATMAN—THE RIDE, Steel Inverted; Level 5   ★★★★★ Super Screamer
3. GREAT AMERICAN SCREAM MACHINE, Steel Looping; Level 5   ★★★★ (When it opened in 1989, this was the tallest and fastest roller coaster in the world.)
4. ROLLING THUNDER, Wood Dual-track Out and Back; Level 3   ★★★
5. RUNAWAY TRAIN, Mine Train; Level 3   ★★★
6. SKULL MOUNTAIN, Enclosed Steel Junior; Level 2   ★★★
7. VIPER, Steel Looping; Level 5   ★★★

Steel Pier, Atlantic City, New Jersey
The original Atlantic City Steel Pier, it now operates as part of Donald Trump's Taj Mahal Resort and Casino.
1. KIDDIE COASTER, Steel Kiddie; Level 1   ★★
2. WILDCAT, Compact Steel; Level 2   ★★

Wonderland Pier, Ocean City, New Jersey (609) 399-7082
1. CITY JET, Compact Steel; Level 2   ★★★

The Great White, Wildwood, N.J., is the first seaside wooden coaster built in almost forty years. (Courtesy of Bobby Nagy)

Batman and Robin—The Chiller. (Courtesy of Six Flags Great Adventure)

New York

Adventureland, East Farmingdale, New York (516) 694-6868
   1. HURRICANE, Steel Junior; Level 2 ★★★

Astroland (at Coney Island), Brooklyn, New York (718) 265-2100
   1. CYCLONE, Wood Twister; Level 5 ★★★★★ Super Screamer
     (The one and only original Coney Island masterpiece, the coaster that
     all others are compared to, much copied and revered.)
   2. BIG APPLE, Steel Kiddie; Level 1 ★★

Coney Island, Brooklyn, New York (718) 372-7099
   1. JUMBO JET, Compact Steel; Level 3 ★★★

Darien Lake Theme Park, Corfu, New York (716) 599-4641
   1. DRAGON, Steel Kiddie; Level 1 ★★
   2. MIND ERASER, Steel Inverted; Level 5 ★★★★
   3. NIGHTMARE, Enclosed Compact Steel; Level 3 ★★★
   4. PREDATOR, Wood Twister; Level 4 ★★★★
   5. VIPER, Steel Looping; Level 4 ★★★

~~~~~~

Roller Coaster Fact: To best display the three-projector wide-screen process known as Cinerama in the film *This Is Cinerama*, a roller coaster was used. The coaster, Atom Smasher (formerly located at Rockaway's Playland in Queens, New York), was a last-minute stand-in. The filmmakers originally intended to use the nearby Coney Island Cyclone, but they found that ride too wild to mount the three cameras needed for the Cinerama process.

~~~~~~

The Great Escape Fun Park, Lake George, New York (518) 792-6568
1. COMET, Wood Out and Back; Level 5   ★★★★★ Super Screamer
   (Originally located in Crystal Beach Amusement Park in Canada, the Comet was moved here in 1994 in the greatest act of roller coaster preservation in history. It's even better now than it was at its first location.)
2. BOOMERANG—COAST TO COASTER, Steel Looping Shuttle; Level 4   ★★★
3. STEAMIN' DEMON, Steel Looping; Level 3   ★★★

Playland, Rye, New York (914) 921-0370
The first totally planned amusement park, now a National Historic Landmark.
1. DRAGON COASTER, Wood Twister; Level 3   ★★★
2. HURRICANE, Steel Junior; Level 3   ★★★
3. KIDDIE COASTER, Wood Kiddie; Level 1   ★★★
   (One of only two wooden kiddie coasters left in the country.)

Sea Breeze, Rochester, New York (716) 323-1900
1. BEAR TRACKS, Steel Kiddie; Level 1   ★★★
2. BOBSLEDS, Steel Junior; Level 2   ★★★
3. JACK RABBIT, Wood Out and Back; Level 3   ★★★★
4. QUANTUM LOOP, Steel Looping; Level 3   ★★★

North Carolina

Ghost Town in the Sky, Maggie Valley, North Carolina (704) 926-1140
1. RED DEVIL, Steel Looping; Level 3   ★★

Comet at Lake George's Great Escape. (Courtesy of Doug Brehm)

Paramount's Carowinds, Charlotte, North Carolina (704) 588-2606
This park literally sits dead center on the North Carolina–South Carolina border. Several of the coasters are positioned so that each ride constitutes an interstate trip!
1. CAROLINA CYCLONE, Steel Looping; Level 3   ★★★
2. CAROLINA GOLD RUSHER, Mine Train; Level 2   ★★★
3. HURLER, Wood Twister; Level 4   ★★★★
   (A movie-themed coaster, situated in the Wayne's World section, named after the Paramount movies.)
4. SCOOBY DOO'S GHOSTER COASTER, Wood Junior; Level 2   ★★★
5. THUNDER ROAD, Wood Dual-track Out and Back; Level 4   ★★★★
   (One side of this racing coaster features trains running backward, offering a different perspective.)
6. VORTEX, Steel Stand-up; Level 4   ★★★★

Ohio

Americana Amusement Park, Middletown, Ohio (513) 539-7339
1. SCREECHIN' EAGLE, Wood Out and Back; Level 3   ★★★
2. SERPENT, Compact Steel; Level 2   ★★★

Cedar Point, Sandusky, Ohio (419) 626-0830
Located on a Lake Erie peninsula, this is the world's best self-contained amusement park, housing more rides than any other, as well as the most

roller coasters of any place in the world. In addition to the amusement park, the peninsula also features several full-service restaurants, a marina, two hotels, a campground, a water park, and beach swimming, all part of the Cedar Point Resort complex.

1. BLUE STREAK, Wood Out and Back; Level 3   ★★★★
2. CEDAR CREEK MINE RIDE, Mine Train; Level 2   ★★★
3. CORKSCREW, Steel Looping; Level 3   ★★★
4. DISASTER TRANSPORT, Enclosed Bobsled; Level 2   ★★★
5. GEMINI, Steel Dual-track Non-looping; Level 4   ★★★★
   (Like Excalibur at sister park Valleyfair!, this ride has a wooden structure and a tubular steel track.)
6. IRON DRAGON, Steel Suspended; Level 2   ★★★
7. JR. GEMINI, Steel Kiddie; Level 1   ★★
8. MAGNUM XL-200, Steel Non-looping; Level 5   ★★★★★ Super Screamer
   (This was the first full-circuit roller coaster with a height of over 200 feet, as well as the first steel coaster of its size to emulate a more traditional wooden coaster. It's all hills, with not a single loop to be found.)
9. MANTIS, Steel Stand-up; Level 5   ★★★★★ Super Screamer
10. MEAN STREAK, Wood Twister; Level 5   ★★★★★ Super Screamer
    (At 161 feet, the world's tallest wooden roller coaster.)
11. RAPTOR, Steel Inverted; Level 5   ★★★★★ Super Screamer
12. WILDCAT, Compact Steel; Level 2   ★★★

Roller Coaster Fact: Cincinnati, Ohio's Coney Island Wildcat served as the inspiration for three modern roller coasters: Wilde Beast at Paramount Canada's Wonderland and the Grizzly rides at Paramount's Kings Dominion and Paramount's Great America.

Geauga Lake, Aurora, Ohio (216) 562-7131
1. BIG DIPPER, Wood Out and Back; Level 3   ★★★★
2. DOUBLE LOOP, Steel Looping; Level 3   ★★★
3. MIND ERASER, Steel Looping Shuttle; Level 4   ★★★
4. RAGING WOLF BOBS, Wood Twister; Level 3   ★★★

Paramount's Kings Island, Cincinnati, Ohio (513) 398-5600
1. ADVENTURE EXPRESS, Mine Train; Level 3   ★★★★
2. BEAST, Wood Terrain; Level 5   ★★★★★ Super Screamer
   (At 7,400 feet, the world's longest wooden roller coaster.)

3. BEASTIE, Wood Junior; Level 2   ★★★
4. KING COBRA, Steel Stand-up; Level 4   ★★★
   (This was the world's first looping stand-up coaster when it opened in 1984.)
5. OUTER LIMITS FLIGHT OF FEAR, Enclosed Steel Looping; Level 5   ★★★★
   (Opened in 1996, the world's first roller coaster to feature a linear induction launch system instead of the traditional lift hill.)
6. RACER, Wood Dual-track Out and Back; Level 3   ★★★★
   (Opening with the park in 1972, this beauty is often credited with reviving interest in the classic wooden roller coaster. One side runs backward.)
7. SCOOBY ZOOM, Steel Kiddie; Level 1   ★★
8. TOP GUN, Steel Suspended; Level 5   ★★★★★ Super Screamer
9. VORTEX, Steel Looping; Level 5   ★★★★

Stricker's Grove, Ross, Ohio (513) 521-9747
Usually open only for private picnics, occasionally to the general public.
1. COMET, Wood Junior; Level 2   ★★★
2. TEDDY BEAR, Steel Kiddie; Level 1   ★★
3. TORNADO, Wood Twister; Level 3   ★★★

Wyandot Lake, Powell, Ohio (614) 889-9283
1. SEA DRAGON, Wood Junior; Level 2   ★★★

Oklahoma

Bell's Amusement Park, Tulsa, Oklahoma (918) 744-1991
1. WILDCAT, Compact Steel; Level 2   ★★
2. ZINGO, Wood Out and Back; Level 3   ★★★
   (Because of neighboring residents' complaints of noise, this coaster does not run after 9:00 P.M. An exception is made when the park becomes the midway for the Oklahoma State Fair.)

Frontier City, Oklahoma City, Oklahoma (405) 478-2412
1. DIAMOND BACK, Steel Looping Shuttle; Level 3   ★★
2. SILVER BULLET, Steel Looping; Level 3   ★★★★
3. WILDCAT, Wood Out and Back; Level 4   ★★

Oregon

Enchanted Forest, Turner, Oregon (503) 363-3060
1. ICE MOUNTAIN BOBSLED, Steel Terrain; Level 2   ★★★

Oaks Amusement Park, Portland, Oregon (503) 233-5777
1. LOOPING STAR, Steel Looping; Level 3 ★★★
2. MONSTER MOUSE, Compact Steel Non-Looping; Level 2 ★★
3. TORNADO, Compact Steel Non-looping; Level 2 ★★

Thrill Ville USA, Turner, Oregon (503) 363-4095
1. RIPPER, Compact Steel; Level 3 ★★★

Pennsylvania

Blands Park, Altoona, Pennsylvania
1. BIG COASTER, Compact Steel; Level 3 ★★★

~~~~~~

Roller Coaster Fact: The Conneaut Lake (Pennsylvania) Blue Streak begins with a dark tunnel, which park personnel call the "Skunk Tunnel" because local skunks take up residence there. Several have been known to find themselves on the track when a train passes through, offering riders an aromatically enhanced ride.

~~~~~~

Conneaut Lake Park, Conneaut Lake Park, Pennsylvania (814) 382-5115
1. BLUE STREAK, Wood Out and Back; Level 4 ★★★

Dorney Park, Allentown, Pennsylvania (610) 395-3724
Open for over 100 years and currently undergoing a modernization, this old park is one of the best places to bring the entire family. It's the best family amusement place in the northeastern United States, as well as one of the best bargains.
1. HERCULES, Wood Terrain; Level 5 ★★★
2. LAZER, Steel Looping; Level 4 ★★★★
3. LITTLE LAZER, Steel Kiddie; Level 1 ★★
4. STEEL FORCE, Steel Non-looping; Level 5 ★★★★★ Super Screamer
   (The tallest roller coaster on the entire Eastern Seaboard.)
5. THUNDER HAWK, Wood Twister; Level 4 ★★★★

Dutch Wonderland, Lancaster, Pennsylvania (717) 291-1888
1. SKY PRINCESS, Wood Out and Back; Level 2 ★★★

Hersheypark, Hershey, Pennsylvania (717) 534-3900
1. COMET, Wood Out and Back; Level 3 ★★★★
2. SIDEWINDER, Steel Looping Shuttle; Level 4 ★★★

Hercules, built into a hillside at Dorney Park, is a good example of a terrain ride. (Courtesy of Dorney Park)

3. SOOPERDOOPERLOOPER, Steel Looping; Level 2   ★★★
4. TRAILBLAZER, Mine Train; Level 2   ★★
5. WILDCAT, Wood Twister; Level 5   ★★★★★ Super Screamer

The Kennywood Racer.
(Courtesy of Bobby Nagy)

Idlewild Park, Ligonier, Pennsylvania (412) 238-3666
1. ROLLO COASTER, Wood Terrain; Level 2   ★★★
2. WILD MOUSE, Steel Junior; Level 3   ★★★

Kennywood, West Mifflin, Pennsylvania (412) 461-0500
This National Historic Landmark is one of the great amusement parks, and one of the finest examples of a classic "traditional" amusement place. The wooden coasters in the park don't copy 1920s classic designs, they are the *originals!*
1. JACK RABBIT, Wood Terrain; Level 2   ★★★
2. LIL' PHANTOM, Steel Kiddie; Level 1   ★★
3. RACER, Wood Dual-track; Level 2   ★★★★
4. STEEL PHANTOM, Steel Looping; Level 5   ★★★★★ Super Screamer
   (The tallest, fastest looping roller coaster in the world.)
5. THUNDERBOLT, Wood Terrain; Level 4   ★★★★

Knoebel's Amusement Resort, Elysburg, Pennsylvania (717) 672-2572
An absolute time-warp. This meticulously clean and well-preserved place is a step back in time; your surroundings and the prices will tell you so.
1. HIGH SPEED THRILL COASTER, Steel Kiddie; Level 3   ★★★★
   (This is indeed a kiddie coaster, but adults are permitted to ride, and when the lift-hill speed is cranked up by the coaster operator, this little demon becomes even wilder than the adult coasters in the park.)
2. PHOENIX, Wood Twister; Level 3   ★★★★
   (The first wooden coaster ever to be relocated and completely rebuilt during modern times.)
3. WHIRLWIND, Steel Looping; Level 3   ★★

Lakemont Park, Altoona, Pennsylvania (814) 949-7275
1. LEAP THE DIPS, Wood Figure Eight; Level 1   ★★★
   (Currently undergoing restoration, this ride dates back more than a century and is the oldest existing roller coaster in the world. This National Historic Landmark is a figure-eight coaster, the style most used in the late nineteenth century.)
2. LITTLE DIPPER, Steel Kiddie; Level 1   ★★
3. MAD MOUSE, Compact Steel; Level 2   ★★
4. SKYLINER, Wood Twister; Level 3   ★★★

Waldameer Park, Erie, Pennsylvania (814) 838-3591
1. COMET JR., Wood Junior; Level 2   ★★★

Williams Grove, Williams Grove, Pennsylvania (717) 697-8266
1. CYCLONE, Wood Out and Back; Level 4   ★★

South Carolina

Family Kingdom, Myrtle Beach, South Carolina (803) 626-3447
1. SWAMP FOX, Wood Out and Back; Level 3   ★★★★

Myrtle Beach Pavilion, Myrtle Beach, South Carolina (803) 448-6456
1. CORKSCREW, Steel Looping; Level 2   ★★
2. GALAXIE, Compact Steet; Level 2   ★★
3. LITTLE EAGLE, Steel Junior; Level 1   ★★

Tennessee

Dollywood, Pigeon Forge, Tennessee (615) 428-9400
Dolly Parton's theme park, one of the most beautiful in the country.
1. BLAZING FURY, Steel Gravity Dark Ride; Level 3   ★★★
2. THUNDER EXPRESS, Mine Train; Level 3   ★★★

Libertyland, Memphis, Tennessee (901) 274-8800
1. REVOLUTION, Steel Looping; Level 3   ★★
2. ZIPPIN PIPPIN, Wood Out and Back; Level 2   ★★★
   (This is not only one of the world's oldest operating coasters, it is also the thrill ride of choice of the late Elvis Presley, who used to rent the ride after hours and ride into the night.)

Opryland, Nashville, Tennessee (615) 889-6600
1. CHAOS, Enclosed Steel Non-Looping; Level 2   ★★★
2. HANGMAN, Steel Inverted; Level 5   ★★★★
3. ROCK 'N' ROLLER COASTER, Mine Train; Level 2   ★★

4. SCREAMIN' DELTA DEMON, Steel Bobsled; Level 2 ★★★
5. WABASH CANNONBALL, Steel Looping; Level 3 ★★

Texas

Sea World of Texas, San Antonio, Texas (210) 523-3000
This marine-life entertainment park, unlike its three other sister parks in Orlando, San Diego, and Cleveland, includes several mechanical rides.
1. GREAT WHITE, Steel Inverted; Level 5 ★★★★★ Super Screamer
(This ride is a duplicate of Batman—The Ride at five of the Six Flags Theme Parks, albeit with aquatic theming. Ironically, none of the three Texas Six Flags parks contain a Batman—The Ride as yet.)

Six Flags Astroworld, Houston, Texas (713) 799-8404
A relatively small park, absolutely jam-packed with a wide variety of roller coasters.
1. BATMAN—THE ESCAPE, Steel Stand-up; Level 5 ★★★★
(Perhaps the most heavily themed thrill ride in the world. The waiting line for this ride practically functions as an attraction in its own right.)
2. EXCALIBUR, Mine Train; Level 3 ★★★
3. GREEZED LIGHTNIN', Steel Looping Shuttle; Level 4 ★★★★
4. MAYAN MINDBENDER, Enclosed Steel Junior; Level 2 ★★★
5. SERPENT, Steel Kiddie; Level 1 ★★
6. TEXAS CYCLONE, Wood Twister; Level 4 ★★★★
(The first-ever copy of the Coney Island Cyclone.)
7. ULTRA TWISTER, Steel Looping; Level 4 ★★★★
(The world's first coaster with vehicles riding between the tracks, it features true heartline spins and one of the steepest drops of any coaster in the world, at a staggering 85 degrees.)
8. VIPER, Steel Looping; Level 3 ★★★★
(This standard looping coaster features a tunnel on the first drop.)
9. XLR-8, Steel Suspended; Level 2 ★★★

Six Flags Fiesta Texas, San Antonio, Texas (210) 697-5050
1. JOKER'S REVENGE, Steel Looping; Level 4 ★★★
(This ride features trains running backward.)
2. PIED PIPER, Steel Junior; Level 1 ★★★
3. RATTLER, Wood Terrain; Level 3 ★★★
4. ROAD RUNNER EXPRESS, Steel Mine Train; Level 3 ★★★★

Six Flags Over Texas, Arlington, Texas (817) 640-8900
This was the first park built by Six Flags, combining the kind of pleasant family attractions associated with Disney parks with more traditional thrill rides. Six Flags introduced the world to many things that are now

Judge Roy Scream, Six Flags Over Texas. (Courtesy of Bobby Nagy)

commonplace within the theme park industry, such as the log flume, the river rapids ride, the tubular steel roller coaster, Broadway-style entertainment, and the pay-one-price admission plan.

1. FLASHBACK, Steel Looping Shuttle; Level 4   ★★★
2. JUDGE ROY SCREAM, Wood Out and Back; Level 3   ★★★
3. LA VIBORA, Steel Bobsled; Level 2   ★★★
4. MINI MINE TRAIN, Steel Kiddie; Level 1   ★★★
5. MR. FREEZE, Steel Looping Shuttle; Level 5   ★★★★
6. RUNAWAY MINE TRAIN, Mine Train; Level 2   ★★★★
   (The world's first mine-train-style coaster.)
7. RUNAWAY MOUNTAIN, Enclosed Steel Junior; Level 3   ★★★
8. SHOCKWAVE, Steel Looping; Level 4   ★★★★
9. TEXAS GIANT, Wood Twister; Level 5   ★★★★★ Super Screamer
   (The undisputed world's number one wooden roller coaster.)

Wonderland, Amarillo, Texas (806) 383-4712
1. BIG COASTER, Compact Steel; Level 2   ★★★
2. CYCLONE, Compact Steel; Level 2   ★★★
3. TEXAS TORNADO, Steel Looping; Level 4   ★★★

Utah

Lagoon, Farmington, Utah (801) 451-0101
1. COLOSSAL FIRE DRAGON, Steel Looping; Level 3   ★★★★
2. JET STAR II, Compact Steel; Level 2   ★★★

Mr. Freeze, making it chillier at two Six Flags parks. A similar design was used for Batman and Robin—The Chiller. (Courtesy of Six Flags Over Texas)

3. PUFF, THE LITTLE FIRE DRAGON, Steel Kiddie; Level 1 ★★
4. ROLLER COASTER, Wood Out and Back; Level 3 ★★★

Virginia

Busch Gardens, Williamsburg, Virginia (804) 253-3000
Often named the most beautiful theme park in the world, its old-world European theming may be even more authentic than Disney's.
1. ALPENGEIST, Steel Inverted; Level 5 ★★★★★ Super Screamer
2. BIG BAD WOLF, Steel Suspended; Level 3 ★★★★
3. DRACHEN FIRE, Steel Looping; Level 5 ★★★★
4. LOCH NESS MONSTER, Steel Looping; Level 4 ★★★★
(One of the most photographed coasters anywhere, with two loops that interlock. Its trains are timed to spin through the loops simultaneously.)
5. WILDE MAUS, Steel Junior; Level 2 ★★★★
(This modern reproduction of the old-style Wild Mouse ride is perhaps the most successful attempt at re-creating an old-fashioned amusement ride experience.)

Paramount's Kings Dominion, Doswell, Virginia (804) 876-5000

One of the nation's best theme parks, containing four wooden roller coasters, more than any other park in the country, and tied with Blackpool Pleasure Beach in England for the most wooden coasters in the entire world.

1. ANACONDA, Steel Looping; Level 4   ★★★★
2. AVALANCHE, Steel Bobsled; Level 2   ★★★★
   (The best bobsled-style coaster in the country, it is also a modern incarnation of the old Flying Turns rides of the 1940s.)
3. GRIZZLY, Wood Twister; Level 5   ★★★★★ Super Screamer
4. HURLER, Wood Twister; Level 4   ★★★★
5. OUTER LIMITS FLIGHT OF FEAR, Enclosed Steel Looping; Level 5   ★★★★
6. REBEL YELL, Wood Dual-track Out and Back; Level 4   ★★★★

Outer Limits Flight of Fear. (Courtesy of Paramount's King Dominion)

    7. SCOOBY DOO, Wood Junior; Level 2   ★★★
    8. SHOCKWAVE, Steel Stand-up; Level 4   ★★★
    9. TAXI JAM, Steel Kiddie; Level 1   ★★★

Washington

Fun Forest, Seattle, Washington (206) 728-1585
    1. WINDSTORM, Steel Junior; Level 3   ★★★

Western Washington Fairgrounds, Puyallup, Washington (206) 845-1771
    1. ROLLER COASTER, Wood Twister; Level 3   ★★★
    (Exclusively a fairground coaster, it only runs for two weeks per year, in late summer.)

West Virginia

Camden Park, Huntington, West Virginia (304) 429-4231
    1. BIG DIPPER, Wood Twister; Level 2   ★★★
    2. LIL' DIPPER, Wood Junior; Level 2   ★★★
    (One of only two wood-track kiddie coasters in the country.)
    3. THUNDERBOLT EXPRESS, Steel Looping Shuttle; Level 3   ★★

Wisconsin

Big Chief Kart and Coaster World, Wisconsin Dells, Wisconsin (608) 254-7858
    Once just a collection of go-kart tracks, this roadside attraction is quickly becoming one of the premier locations of wooden roller coasters.
    1. CYCLOPS, Wood Terrain; Level 3   ★★★★
    2. PEGASUS, Wood Junior; Level 2   ★★★
    3. ZEUS, Wood Out and Back; Level 4   ★★★★

Little A-Merrick-A, Marshall, Wisconsin
    1. LITTLE DIPPER, Steel Kiddie; Level 1   ★★
    2. MAD MOUSE, Compact Steel; Level 2   ★★

SOUTH AMERICA

ARGENTINA

Interama, Buenos Aires
    1. RACER, Steel Dual-track Non-looping; Level 3   ★★★★

BRAZIL

Play Centre, São Paolo
    1. DOUBLE LOOP, Steel Looping; Level 3   ★★★
    2. LA FONTE IMPRESSA, Steel Junior; Level 2   ★★

9 THE BEST ROLLER COASTER TRIPS

Roller coaster fans worldwide have been known to plan entire vacations centered around amusement parks and roller coasters.

Following are some suggested park combinations that will create coaster-oriented vacations lasting anywhere from a long weekend to a week or two. All are flexible and may be added to or shortened to form a trip tailor-made to fulfill your needs.

In most cases, your trip will require hotel stays. Some parks have adjacent hotels; many parks are complete resorts with hotels on the property (these are noted in the trip descriptions). Call the park for information on nearby accommodations.

Many major hotel chains have locations near individual parks. They may be reached by calling the following 800 numbers:

Best Western	1-800-528-1234
Choice Hotels International (including Sleep Inn, Comfort Inn, Quality Inn, Clarion, and Friendship)	1-800-424-6423
Days Inn	1-800-325-2525
Econo Lodge	1-800-446-6900
Hilton Hotels	1-800-445-8667
Holiday Inn	1-800-465-4329
Howard Johnson	1-800-654-4329
Hyatt Hotels	1-800-233-1234
Knights Inn	1-800-843-5644
La Quinta	1-800-531-5900

Marriott Hotels	1-800-228-9290
Motel 6	1-800-466-8356
Radisson Hotels	1-800-333-3333
Ramada Inn	1-800-272-6232
Red Roof	1-800-THE-ROOF
Rodeway Inn	1-800-228-2660
Sheraton	1-800-325-3535
Stouffer Hotels	1-800-468-3571
Super 8 Motels	1-800-800-8000

THE WEST COASTER

*Includes Six Flags Magic Mountain, Disneyland,
Knott's Berry Farm and Belmont Park.*

Travel Information

Airport: If flying, use Los Angeles International Airport.
Hotel: Southern California is all about driving cars. It is also a major tourist center, with any number of things to do that have nothing to do with theme parks. It is therefore suggested that you center yourself at one hotel for the duration of your stay in Southern California.

All four parks are conveniently located just off I-5, and all are open year-round.

Six Flags Magic Mountain, Valencia, California

Located just north of Los Angeles. Take the Magic Mountain exit off I-5. The park is visible from the highway.

Part of the Six Flags California complex (which also includes a great water park known as Six Flags Hurricane Harbor), Six Flags is home to the largest collection of roller coasters in the western United States, including top thrillers Superman—The Escape, Batman—The Ride, Viper, and Psyclone.

During the winter, early spring, and late fall, the park is only open on weekends and holidays.

TIPS FOR THIS PARK: Upon entering the main gate, most guests will head for the Viper or Revolution, located near the entrance, or straight up to the top of Samurai Summit, the location of the awesome Superman—The Escape. Go to Colossus first, then work your way around the park in

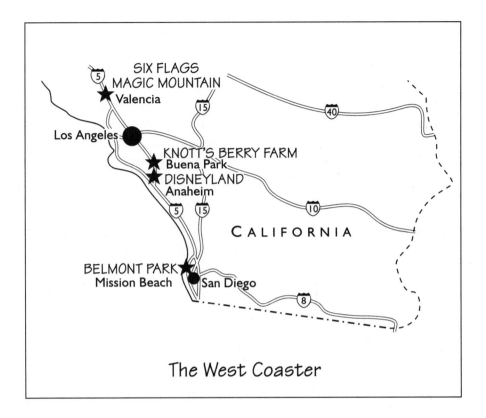

The West Coaster

a counterclockwise pattern. By the time you've returned to your starting point, the lines for the coasters nearest the main gate should be shorter.

If you just want to ride the coasters, one day is all it will take (if the park is crowded, that's all you may get to do). If you want to experience all the rest the park has to offer, a two-day visit is recommended.

Knott's Berry Farm, Buena Park, California

In Buena Park, take the Beach Boulevard exit off I-5.

Knott's Berry Farm is home to five roller coasters. Its newest is the Windjammer, a dual-track steel loop racing coaster.

TIPS FOR THIS PARK: The park attracts a family crowd, so lines on the more intense coasters are not usually a problem. Go during the week to avoid crowds. A one-day visit should give you your fill, but if you enjoy shows, shopping, and the like, you might want to plan accordingly.

Disneyland, Anaheim, California

Take the Harbor Boulevard exit off I-5. NOTE: Redevelopment of the Disneyland property includes plans to create a new exit off the interstate that will lead directly to the resort, which will include a new theme park, California Adventures.

The first full-fledged theme park in the world is home to four coasters, all of them suitable for any member of the family.

Disneyland is a complete resort, with hotels located directly on the property. It provides a good base location for your West Coaster trip.

TIPS FOR THIS PARK: Disneyland gets more visitors than any other park in the country. It's always crowded, but lines move fast. Try going on a day when the park is open until midnight, and get there as soon as the gates open. Head to the Matterhorn first thing, and save Gadget's Go Coaster for the nighttime, when most of the kiddies have gone home.

Roller Coaster Fact: Building Big Thunder Mountain Railroad at Disneyland in 1979 cost almost as much as building the entire park back in 1955.

Belmont Park, San Diego, California

Take I-5 to San Diego. Take the Sea World exit, and follow the road into Mission Beach.

Once a fully operational amusement park, it is now a shopping plaza that includes a classic wooden roller coaster.

TIPS FOR THIS PARK: Since it's not exactly a full amusement park, buy your tickets and ride at your leisure. Be sure to take a stroll on the beach.

VIRGINIA IS FOR ROLLER COASTER LOVERS

Includes Busch Gardens, Williamsburg, Paramount's Kings Dominion, and Adventure World.

Travel Information

Airport: Fly into either Richmond International or Dulles International.
Hotel: Because the parks are several hours from each other, it is recommended that you book hotels near the parks.

All the parks are easily accessible from I-95, a major East Coast north-south route.

Busch Gardens, Williamsburg, Williamsburg, Virginia

Take I-95 to I-295 (in Richmond) to I-64. Exit I-64 at exit 242. Follow signs to Route 60, and to the park.

Most major hotel chains have locations throughout the Williamsburg area.

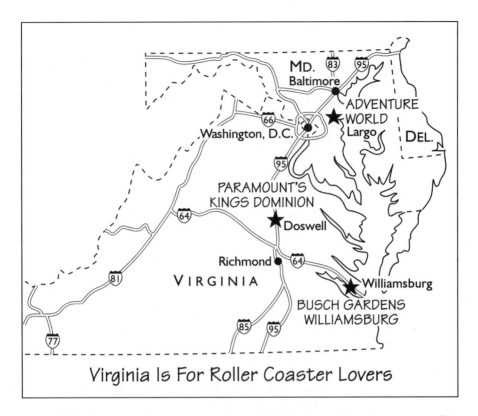

Virginia Is For Roller Coaster Lovers

Widely regarded as the most beautiful theme park in the country, this park is themed to old-world European countries.

Roller coasters include the famous Loch Ness Monster, Big Bad Wolf, and Alpengeist, the park's newest and most intense thriller.

TIPS FOR THIS PARK: Unless it has no line, bypass Loch Ness Monster, which is right in the front of the park, and head back to the themed area known as Oktoberfest, where three of the park's coasters are located. Head back to Loch Ness in the afternoon, when lines will be shortest.

Paramount's Kings Dominion, Doswell, Virginia

Located directly off I-95, at exit 98.

One of the Paramount Parks, and home to four wooden roller coasters, the most in North America.

The Best Western Kings Quarters Hotel is located adjacent to the park, with others throughout the area.

TIPS FOR THIS PARK: Wherever else you head, first hop on the stand-up Shockwave; because of a slow loading process, it always has the most unbearably long and sluggish line in the park. Then head right on back to the Congo section, home to Avalanche, Outer Limits Flight of Fear, and Anaconda. At the end of the day, the lines will usually be short on Grizzly, Hurler, and Rebel Yell.

Adventure World, Largo, Maryland

In Maryland, take exit 15 off I-95/495. Follow Route 214 to the park.

One of Premier Parks' thirteen North American theme parks, it features the fierce wooden Wild One and the inverted Mind Eraser.

Hotels are located throughout the Washington, D.C., area.

TIPS FOR THIS PARK: Go right to the Python and Wild One and ride them first thing, as each only operates one train and has a low capacity.

THE EIGHTEEN FLAGS OVER TEXAS TOUR

Includes Six Flags Over Texas, Six Flags Astroworld, and Six Flags Fiesta Texas

Travel Information

Airport: Use any of the airports located in the cities containing the parks. *Hotel:* Because of the travel time between parks, it is essential to book hotels located near each park.

It is also essential to purchase a Six Flags season pass at whatever park you first attend. The pass will admit you to all three parks, plus any other Six Flags parks you happen upon during your travels.

Six Flags Over Texas, Arlington, Texas

Located midway between Dallas and Fort Worth, off Interstate 30.

This park is the first one built by the Six Flags Theme Park Company. It is one of their best and contains the world's number one wooden roller coaster, the Texas Giant.

Although there are dozens of hotels and motels throughout the area, the most convenient is the La Quinta Inn, located directly across the street from the park's entrance. Ask for a room with a view of the park; you'll wake up in the morning to the sound of roller coasters rumbling their way through their daily test runs. You'll also be able to walk to the park.

Roller Coaster Fact: The Six Flags Over Texas Shock Wave was the first roller coaster to feature two consecutive loops. The loops, each 70 feet high, are positioned next to a freeway running adjacent to the park. For a long time after the ride's debut, the loops were responsible for many car accidents.

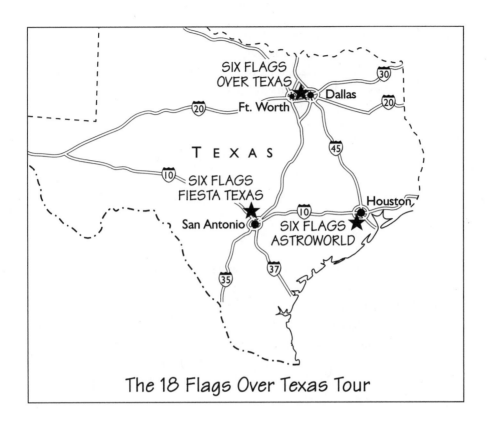

The 18 Flags Over Texas Tour

TIPS FOR THIS PARK: Head to the Texas Giant first—it's the park's most popular ride.

Six Flags Astroworld, Houston, Texas
Located adjacent to the Astrodome, off the I-610 Loop.

After Six Flags built its first three parks, it began buying parks already in existence, starting with this one. It contains nine roller coasters, including the Texas Cyclone, the original copy of the Coney Island Cyclone.

Major hotel chains are located throughout the area. Several are part of the Astro Village, located directly across the street from the parking lot that serves both Six Flags Astroworld and the Astrodome. Call the park for all the details.

Six Flags Fiesta Texas, San Antonio, Texas
Take Exit 556 off I-10.

Located in an abandoned quarry, the park was recently added to the Six Flags family of parks. Its major roller coaster is the Rattler, a wooden ride that scales the quarry walls.

Hotels and motels are located throughout the San Antonio metro area.

TIPS FOR THIS PARK: This is basically a show park, with several major thrill rides (since Six Flags took over, more thrill rides are in the planning stages). Those looking for thrills flock to the major rides, and lines can be long. Ride the coasters first thing in the morning.

THE OHIO IS ROLLER COASTER COUNTRY TOUR

Includes Cedar Point, Geauga Lake, and Paramount's Kings Island

Travel Information

Airport: While Cedar Point and Geauga Lake are located near Cleveland, Paramount's Kings Island is just north of Cincinnati. Use either Cleveland Hopkins International or, for a more centrally located airport, Columbus International.

Hotel: Although fine hotels are located near Geauga Lake, it is probably better to base yourself out of a hotel located near Cedar Point when visiting those two parks. A separate hotel is required for Paramount's Kings Island, located about four hours to the south.

Cedar Point, Sandusky, Ohio

Take exit 7 off I-80 (the Ohio Turnpike). Follow Route 250 into Sandusky, and follow the clearly marked signs to the park.

Cedar Point is a complete resort located on a Lake Erie peninsula. It contains the greatest collection of roller coasters in the world, a total of twelve.

Cedar Point has two hotels located on the peninsula, directly adjacent to the amusement park. These, of course, are the most convenient. The park also owns the Radisson Harbor Hotel, located at the entrance to the Cedar Point causeway. Dozens of additional motels are located throughout this resort town. (This author swears by the Maples Motel, 419-626-1575, located directly between the two entrances to the Cedar Point peninsula. It's simple but extremely comfortable, and it caters to a pleas-

---

Roller Coaster Fact: The Corkscrew at Cedar Point was the world's first roller coaster that featured three upside-down elements.

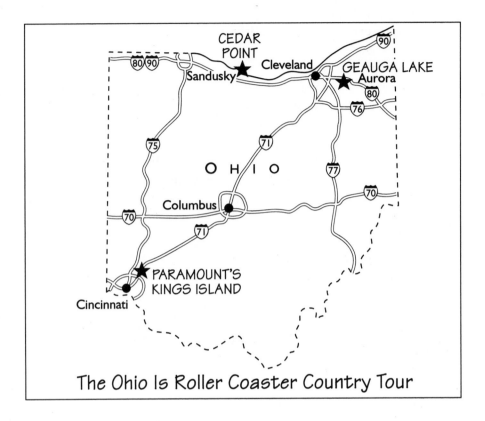

The Ohio Is Roller Coaster Country Tour

ant clientele, many of whom have been coming back for years. Owners Joan and Ken Faber will look after you like your own mother would.)

TIPS FOR THIS PARK: Get to the park early. Lines get extremely long on all the rides, but try riding Mean Streak first, and work your way to the front of the park. Raptor, located immediately inside the front gate, will have its shortest line in the afternoon; it's the first and last thing most park guests ride. One other thing—this park closes its major roller coasters at even the slightest hint of rain. While a few may indeed be operating, it is doubtful that they'll be the ones you came to the park especially to ride. To make matters worse, since this is a resort park, rain does not deter the crowds, either. Plan your visit for a sunny day, if possible during the week in early May or the last week in August, when crowds are at their lightest. Whenever you go, two days are necessary to do everything the park and resort have to offer.

Geauga Lake, Aurora, Ohio

From I-80, take exit 13 onto I-480. Exit in Twinsburg onto Route 91 north. Take that to Solon, then turn right onto Route 42 to the park, which will be on your left. NOTE: The towns of Solon and Aurora are notorious speed traps! Do not drive even slightly over the posted speed limits, which, by the way, fluctuate greatly and frequently on Route 42 near the park.

Geauga Lake is a classic traditional amusement park, recently purchased by the Premier Parks chain and now undergoing an expansion and refurbishment. It is home to the Big Dipper, a classic 1920s John Miller ride, and the Raging Wolf Bobs, a new ride patterned after the infamous Riverview Bobs, formerly located in Chicago.

TIPS FOR THIS PARK: Lines on the Big Dipper are shortest early and late in the day. The Raging Wolf Bobs has longest lines in the middle of the day.

Paramount's Kings Island, Kings Island (Cincinnati), Ohio

Take exit 25 off I-71, and follow the signs to the park, which is visible from the highway.

The star park in the Paramount Parks chain is also the best theme park of its kind in the country. Among its coaster lineup is the Beast, the longest wooden roller coaster in the world.

The Kings Island Inn is located directly across the service road from the park. There is also an adjacent campground. Other accommodations are located throughout the area.

TIPS FOR THIS PARK: Get thee to the Beast, first thing! Be warned, however, that this is a popular night ride, and lines will continue to be long right up to park closing.

During this particular trip, you may also want to visit Wyandot Lake, a small amusement/water park adjacent to the Columbus Zoo, in Powell, Ohio, a Columbus suburb. The park is owned by Premier Parks, so if you've purchased a Premier Parks season pass, your admission is already taken care of. The park has a rare junior wooden coaster built in the late 1950s.

THE HOOSIER/SLUGGER TOUR

Includes Kentucky Kingdom, Holiday World, and Indiana Beach.

Travel Information

Airport: Use Louisville International.

Hotel: Stay at any of the many motels located throughout the Louisville area for both Kentucky Kingdom and Holiday World. Indiana Beach is a full resort with hotels and rental cottages located directly within the amusement park.

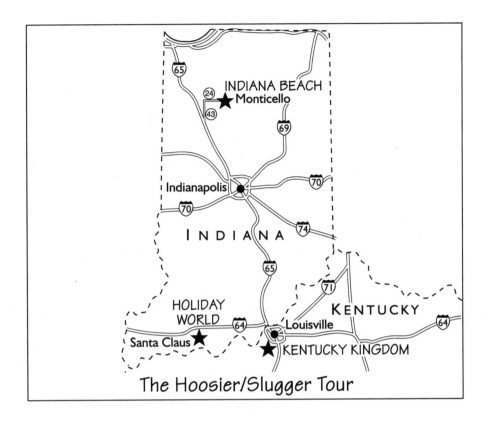

The Hoosier/Slugger Tour

Kentucky Kingdom, Louisville, Kentucky

Located adjacent to the Kentucky Fair and Exposition Center, exit 11 off I-264.

Chock-filled with thrill rides, this park is home to Chang, the world's longest, tallest, and fastest stand-up coaster.

TIPS FOR THIS PARK: A service road cuts through the center of the park, with a single bridge the only access from one half of the park to the other. While most of the best rides in the park are indeed on one side, they are unfortunately not on the side that contains the park entrance and most of the other attractions. It is a long walk to and over the bridge; once you've made it over there, plan on staying for a while. (Park management plans on correcting this awkward situation in years to come.)

Holiday World, Santa Claus, Indiana

Take exit 63 off I-64. Follow Route 162 to the park.

This family theme park has been in operation longer than Disneyland and bills itself as the nation's oldest theme park. It is home to the Raven, a highly recommended, thrilling wooden roller coaster.

TIPS FOR THIS PARK: Lines do not get unmanageable at this park, which is divided into Christmas, Halloween, and Fourth of July themed areas.

Try to schedule your visit for when the park is open past sunset—night rides on the Raven are amazing!

Indiana Beach, Monticello, Indiana

Take exit 178 off I-65. Follow Route 43 north to Route 24 east, into Monticello. Follow signs to the resort.

This true old-fashioned boardwalk amusement area, located directly on Lake Shafer, is home to the Hoosier Hurricane, a wonderful woodie built over and around other park attractions, as well as over the lake.

The resort has its own hotel, as well as large cottages for rent. Several days could be spent here, enjoying not only the rides but also the restaurants, the beach, the water sports, and the nightlife—yes, the park has a nightclub, with live entertainment.

TIPS FOR THIS PARK: The park has two parking lots, one of which is located almost under the Hoosier Hurricane's loading station. If you are day-tripping, try the other lot; to get to the park, you must traverse a suspension bridge across part of the lake—at one point, the Hurricane dives *under* the bridge. The park offers two pay-one-price sessions; late afternoon, when these sessions overlap, actually offers the least crowded moments of the day.

MISSOURI, THE "SHOW ME ROLLER COASTERS" STATE TOUR

Includes Six Flags St. Louis and Worlds of Fun

Travel Information

Airport: Use either St. Louis International or Kansas City International.
Hotel: It's a long drive between the parks. Hotels and motels are located within minutes of each. It is possible, but not recommended, to base yourself out of one hotel for both.

Six Flags St. Louis, Allenton, Missouri

Take exit 261 off I-44. The park is visible from the highway.

The latest park actually built by Six Flags, it is also one of its best and most beautiful, situated on a hillside. The world-renowned Screamin' Eagle spans the topmost reaches of the park.

A Ramada Inn is located adjacent to the park and provides shuttle service to the main gate.

TIPS FOR THIS PARK: Crowds will head directly for Batman—The Ride first thing in the morning. Head directly up the hill to the Screamin' Eagle, and you'll be able to enjoy it well before everyone else gets there;

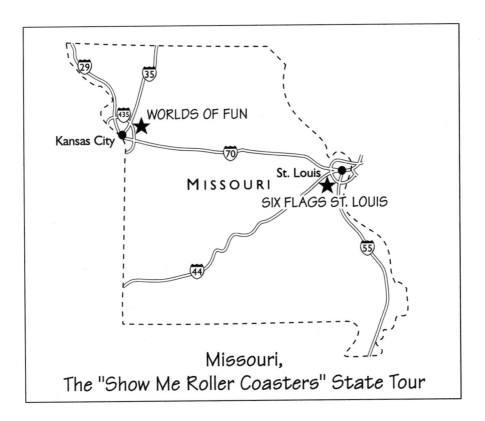

Missouri,
The "Show Me Roller Coasters" State Tour

it will also have shorter lines just prior to park closing. Batman will have shorter lines in the middle of the day.

Worlds of Fun, Kansas City, Missouri

Located off exit 53 on I-435, the park is visible from the highway.

Owned and operated by Cedar Fair, LP, this park is themed after the countries featured in *Around the World in Eighty Days*. It is home to three world-class roller coasters, including the highly rated Timber Wolf.

TIPS FOR THIS PARK: Lines here are spread pretty evenly throughout the day, but Zambezi Zinger, located in the back of the park, will probably have its shortest early and late in the day. Night rides on this Anton Schwarzkopf masterpiece are recommended.

THE KEYSTONE COASTER TOUR

Includes Kennywood, Hersheypark, and Dorney Park

Travel Information

Airport: To be centrally located, fly into Harrisburg International Airport. *Hotel:* You'll require two—one in the Harrisburg area, and one in the Pittsburgh area.

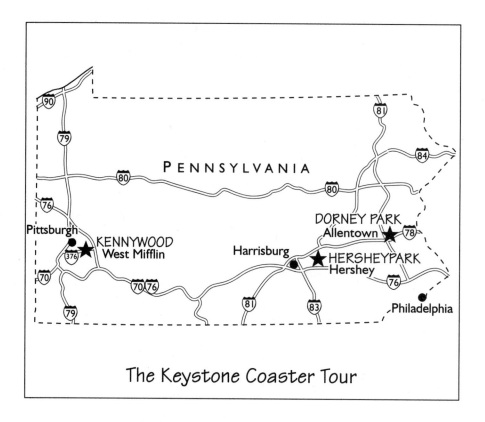

The Keystone Coaster Tour

Kennywood, West Mifflin, Pennsylvania

Take exit 6 off I-76 (the Pennsylvania Turnpike), onto I-376. Take that to exit 9 (Swissvale). From there, it gets a bit complicated, as you'll be driving through residential neighborhoods, but keep a sharp lookout for the bright yellow Kennywood Park arrows, which will point the way. As you cross the Monongahela River, you'll see the park to your left, sitting on top of a bluff overlooking the water.

Kennywood is a fine traditional park, with classic amusement rides next to modern computer-driven thrillers. The park is home to three classic wooden coasters, all originally built in the 1920s, and the Steel Phantom, the tallest and fastest looping steel roller coaster in the world.

TIPS FOR THIS PARK: The longest line in the park is usually for the Steel Phantom; it's also the slowest moving. If you are interested in the fastest-moving line possible, do not ride the Phantom early or late in the day, as the park is famous for running only one train on the Phantom at those times, no matter how long the lines are. The park also tends to end multiple-train operation well before the park closes for the evening. Don't be afraid of what appear to be long lines on any of the coasters when they are running at full capacity; the waiting time will be surprisingly short.

Roller Coaster Fact:　Several Roaring Twenties roller coasters have been designated National Historic Landmarks: the Giant Dippers in Santa Cruz and San Diego, California; Jack Rabbit, Racer, and Thunderbolt, at Kennywood (near Pittsburgh, Pennsylvania); Dragon and Kiddie Coasters, at Playland, (Rye, New York); and the Cyclone at Coney Island (Brooklyn, New York).

Hersheypark, Hershey, Pennsylvania

Use either exit 27 or 28 off I-81, and follow signs to the park.

This full resort is home to five coasters, including the Wildcat, patterned after classic 1920s rip-roaring designs.

The Hotel Hershey and Hershey Lodge are located adjacent to the park, with major hotel and motel chains throughout the area.

TIPS FOR THIS PARK: Try heading to the Wildcat first thing. You might also want to hop on the low-capacity Sidewinder before things get too hectic. This park gets very crowded with large families. Attempt to schedule your visit for a weekday or Sunday, when crowds tend to be smaller.

Dorney Park, Allentown, Pennsylvania

Take I-78 to exit 16 (if traveling east) or 17 (if traveling west) onto Hamilton Boulevard. The park is visible from the exit.

If you want tall roller coasters, this is the park for you! Dorney is currently home to the tallest wood and tallest steel coasters on the East Coast.

TIPS FOR THIS PARK: Because of adjacent water park Wildwater Kingdom, the amusement park section has its smallest crowds before early evening. Try not to gawk too much when you exit the highway—the 200-foot-tall Steel Force, spanning the back of the park from one end to the other, completely dominates the place. Head right for it (but not when you're driving—wait until you get into the park!); lines will be long on this baby all day.

NEW JERSEY COASTLINE COASTERS

Includes Six Flags Great Adventure and Morey's Piers

Travel Information

Airport: Use Newark International Airport.

Hotel: There are no hotels located nearer than fifteen miles to Six Flags. Morey's Piers are located in the Wildwoods, a major beach resort with

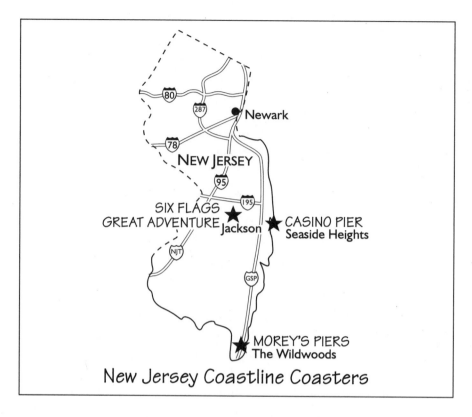

New Jersey Coastline Coasters

hundreds of privately owned motels, a few of which are the luxury resort type. Call the park for exact recommendations. NOTE: The hotels in the Wildwoods are expensive and usually require a minimum stay of two or three nights.

Six Flags Great Adventure, Jackson, New Jersey

Take exit 7A off the New Jersey Turnpike, or exit 98 from the Garden State Parkway, both of which lead to I-195. Take that to exit 16 (Route 537), and follow the signs. The park entrance will be on your right. You won't see anything of the park itself until you're in the parking lot.

This is Six Flags' largest park, and it has the highest attendance of any seasonal park in the country. The stand-out attractions are Batman—The Ride and Batman and Robin—The Chiller, which is the park's tallest roller coaster, at 200 feet.

TIPS FOR THIS PARK: First and foremost, avoid this park like the plague on Saturdays during the summer—it can get too crowded for its own good. Once inside the main gate, head for the fountain and turn left (most guests will head to the superhero thrill rides located to the right of the entrance). Make your way to the Frontier Adventure section of the park and try the three coasters in this area; they won't have severe lines until much later in the day.

Morey's Piers, The Wildwoods, New Jersey

Take exit 6 off the Garden State Parkway, and follow Route 147 into town. NOTE: Daily parking can get expensive the closer to the boardwalk you go. Look around for a lot that fits your budget, but beware—some lots charge for parking sessions, so be sure that the price you are being charged is for the full time of your planned visit before you commit to parking there. Also, the three piers that are part of Morey's are pretty well spread out, so you may want to park somewhere between the two that are furthest from each other.

TIPS FOR THIS PARK: A day at the Wildwoods boardwalk will require a lot of walking. Morey's Pier is located in North Wildwood, while Mariner's Landing and Wild Wheels Pier are in Wildwood, with Wild Wheels almost at the border of Wildwood Crest. A pay-one-price wristband is good for all three, plus time in a water park when in season (a must on weekends, when the combo pass is the only one available for sale). No matter how crowded the resort town gets, the piers will not be crowded during the day, when most people are either on the beach or in the water parks. At night, however, the piers will get very crowded, and the lines long. The good side to this is that the piers will stay open as long as the crowds last, sometimes until 2:00 A.M. This is especially good news for fans of wooden roller coasters, as Wild Wheels Pier's Great White turns from a great ride during the day into an absolute monster machine (one that takes no prisoners) at night.

On your way back north, don't forget to stop at the other great boardwalk piers dotting the New Jersey coast. They contain the best collection of compact steel roller coasters in the world. Don't miss the Jet Star on Casino Pier in Seaside Heights. It's located at the end of the pier over the ocean and can be terrifying to some.

THE LAKE RIVER ESCAPE

Includes Lake Compounce, Riverside Park,
and The Great Escape Fun Park

Travel Information

Airport: Fly into Bradley International, north of Hartford, Connecticut.
Hotel: You'll need two: one near Riverside in Massachusetts and one near the Great Escape in the Lake George, New York, vicinity.

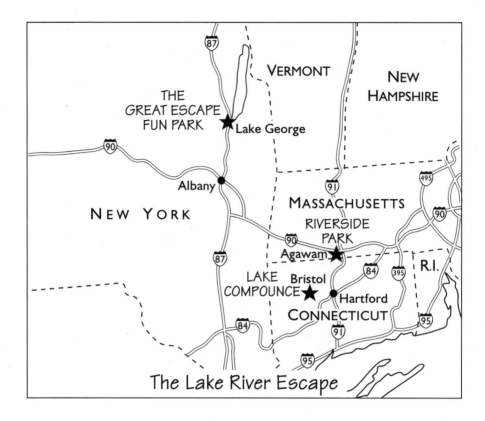

The Lake River Escape

Lake Compounce, Bristol, Connecticut

Take I-84 to exit 31. Follow signs to Bristol and the park.

Lake Compounce is the oldest operating amusement park in the United States. It has recently been purchased by the Kennywood Corporation, and new rides and renovation are the order of the day. Its major roller coaster is the wooden Wildcat, built in 1927 and completely reconstructed in 1986.

TIPS FOR THIS PARK: This is an old park, but it is being completely restored, with many new rides and attractions. Plan to spend a leisurely day, absorbing the atmosphere.

Riverside Park, Agawam, Massachusetts

Take exit 47 west off I-91. Take Route 190 to Route 159. Turn right onto 159, and follow the road to the park, which will appear on your right as soon as you have crossed into Massachusetts.

Recently purchased by the Premier Parks chain, Riverside is currently undergoing a massive renovation, which will include a new entrance and many new rides. The park's Riverside Cyclone is one of the most diabolical wooden roller coasters in the world.

TIPS FOR THIS PARK: Ride the coasters early in the day. The lines move slowly at this park and stay long until closing. Additionally, the Cyclone is a rough ride, and its trains are completely made of unforgiving, uncushioned fiberglass, a drawback that the new owners will hopefully soon correct. Until then, if you don't want your butt kicked, sit nearer the front, and always in the front portion of one of the six cars that connect to make the full train. (If you do like your coasters rambunctious, by all means head for the back seat—you won't be disappointed.) Be warned, however, that the park has severe "No Choice of Seat" rules on all its coasters. If you wind up in a seat you think you can't handle, tell them. Complain at Guest Services, write letters, etc., until they change the rule.

A season pass purchased at Riverside is also good for admission to the Great Escape, as both are members of the Premier Parks family.

The Great Escape Fun Park, Lake George, New York

Take exit 19 off I-87. Go to Route 9, turn left, and follow the road to the park.

The park began life as Storytown USA and was recently purchased by the Premier Parks chain. It is home to the Comet, one of the best roller coasters in the world.

There are dozens of hotels in the Lake George resort area. Several are located directly across the road from the park.

TIPS FOR THIS PARK: Lines for the Comet are longest midday. Ride first thing in the morning and toward park closing. The steel looping Steamin' Demon rarely has a significant line.

THE GREAT LAKES COASTER TOUR

Includes Sea Breeze, Darien Lake,
and Paramount Canada's Wonderland

Travel Information

Airport: Use Buffalo International Airport.
Hotel: Darien Lake, located about midway between the two other parks, offers RV rentals in its huge campground, which is located adjacent to the amusement park. Try that, or any of the major chain hotels and motels throughout the Buffalo area.

Sea Breeze, Rochester, New York

From I-90, take either exit 45 or 47 onto I-490. Take that to Route 590 (the Sea Breeze Expressway). The park is at the end of the expressway, on Culver Road.

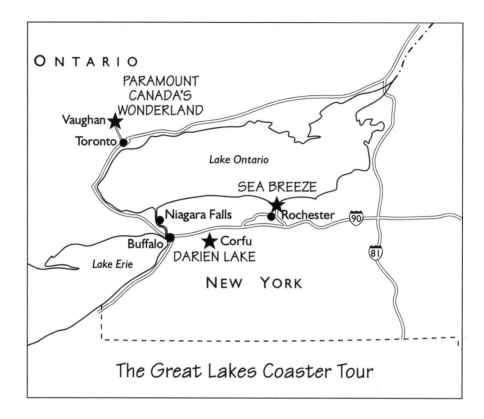

The Great Lakes Coaster Tour

Sea Breeze is a classic traditional park, with several unique coasters and attractions.

TIPS FOR THIS PARK: If possible, do not ride the Jack Rabbit until night-time. The ride is filled with surprises that work much better in the darkness. Trivia hounds will be interested to know that the steepest drop in the park belongs to the Log Flume, which was purchased and moved from the long-gone Euclid Beach Amusement Park in Cleveland, Ohio.

Darien Lake, Corfu, New York

A large amusement park plus camping resort, it is home to New York State's tallest wooden roller coaster, as well as to its only enclosed coaster.

TIPS FOR THIS PARK: The park may get very crowded. Head right for the low-capacity Nightmare indoor coaster. The wooden Predator will have its shortest lines midday, as it is located near the main entrance.

Paramount Canada's Wonderland, Vaughan, Ontario, Canada

From the United States, take I-90 to I-190 into Canada. Follow the signs to the Queen Elizabeth Way, all the way to Toronto. The park is accessible from either Route 400 or Route 404, just north of Toronto.

You must pass through customs both entering Canada and returning to the United States. Although a passport is not required, it is the best form of identification when traveling to other countries. At the very least, carry your birth certificate and a photo ID. Unless you purchase over $500 worth of souvenirs at the park, you do not have to declare them to customs.

Paramount Canada's Wonderland accepts American currency for admission and all purchases. The cash registers will compute the rate of exchange, but please be aware that your change for purchases will be given to you in Canadian currency.

A member of the Paramount Parks chain, the park features the largest collection of roller coasters in Canada, and one of the greatest varieties of coasters in the world.

TIPS FOR THIS PARK: Try to schedule your visit to this park during the week on what is a holiday in the United States that is not celebrated in Canada (for example: Memorial Day and Independence Day). The park can get extremely busy on weekends and Canadian holidays. Most of the park's coasters line the back of the park; start with the Mighty Canadian Minebuster and work your way across. Ride the inverted Top Gun during midday, since it is located next to the entrance and will have its shortest lines at that time.

10 THE WORLD'S MAJOR WOOD COASTERS

(Listed alphabetically, by continent. Listing includes the name of the ride, the park, and the country. Check off in the box provided each roller coaster that you have ridden.)

ASIA

- ❑ Jupiter   Kijima Resort, Japan
- ❑ Little Dipper   Esselworld, India
- ❑ White Canyon   Yomiuriland, Japan
- ❑ White Cyclone   Nagashima Spaland, Japan

AUSTRALIA

- ❑ Beastie   Australia's Wonderland, Australia
- ❑ Bush Beast   Australia's Wonderland, Australia
- ❑ Scenic Railway   Luna Park, Australia

EUROPE

- ❑ Anaconda   Walibi Stroumpf, France
- ❑ Antelope   Gulliver's World, England
- ❑ Big Dipper   Blackpool Pleasure Beach, England
- ❑ Cyclone   Southport Pleasure Beach, England
- ❑ Grand National   Blackpool Pleasure Beach, England
- ❑ Hullamvasit   Vidam Park, Hungary

❑ MegaFobia	Oakwood Leisure Park, Wales
❑ Pegasus	De Eftelling, The Netherlands
❑ Roller Coaster	Blackpool Pleasure Beach, England
❑ Roller Coaster	Great Yarmouth Pleasure Beach, England
❑ Runaway Mine Train	Frontier Land, England
❑ Rutschebanen	Bakken, Denmark
❑ Rutschebanen	Tivoli Gardens, Denmark
❑ Scenic Railway	Dreamland Fun Park, England
❑ Sierra Tonante	Mirabilandia, Italy
❑ Stampida	Port Aventura, Spain
❑ Texas Tornado	Frontier Land, England
❑ Tomahawk	Port Aventura, Spain
❑ Tonerre de Zeus	Parc Astérix, France
❑ Wild Mouse	Blackpool Pleasure Beach, England
❑ Vuoristorata	Linnanmaki Park, Finland
❑ Zipper Dipper	Blackpool Pleasure Beach, England

NORTH AMERICA

(These listings also include the state or province, where applicable.)

❑ American Eagle	Six Flags Great America, Illinois, USA
❑ Beast	Paramount's Kings Island, Ohio, USA
❑ Beastie	Paramount's Kings Island, Ohio, USA
❑ Big Dipper	Camden Park, West Virginia, USA
❑ Big Dipper	Geauga Lake, Ohio, USA
❑ Blue Streak	Cedar Point, Ohio, USA
❑ Blue Streak	Conneaut Lake Park, Pennsylvania, USA
❑ Cannonball	Waterville, USA, Alabama, USA
❑ Colossus	Six Flags Magic Mountain, California, USA
❑ Comet	The Great Escape, New York, USA
❑ Comet	Hersheypark, Pennsylvania, USA
❑ Comet	Stricker's Grove, Ohio, USA
❑ Comet Jr.	Waldameer Park, Pennsylvania, USA
❑ Cyclone	Astroland, New York, USA
❑ Cyclone	Lakeside Park, Colorado, USA
❑ Cyclone	Williams Grove, Pennsylvania, USA
❑ Cyclops	Big Chief, Wisconsin, USA
❑ Dragon Coaster	Playland, New York, USA
❑ Flyer Comet	Whalom Park, Massachusetts, USA
❑ Georgia Cyclone	Six Flags Over Georgia, Georgia, USA

❏ Ghoster Coaster — Paramount Canada's Wonderland, Ontario, Canada

❏ Giant Coaster — Arnolds Park, Iowa, USA

❏ Giant Dipper — Belmont Park, California, USA

❏ Giant Dipper — Santa Cruz Beach Boardwalk, California, USA

❏ Great American Scream Machine — Six Flags Over Georgia, Georgia, USA

❏ Great White — Wild Wheels Pier, New Jersey, USA

❏ Grizzly — Paramount's Great America, California, USA

❏ Grizzly — Paramount's Kings Dominion, Virginia, USA

❏ Grizzly — Silverwood Theme Park, Idaho, USA

❏ Hercules — Dorney Park, Pennsylvania, USA

❏ High Roller — Valleyfair!, Minnesota, USA

❏ Hoosier Hurricane — Indiana Beach, Indiana, USA

❏ Hurler — Paramount's Carowinds, North Carolina, USA

❏ Hurler — Paramount's Kings Dominion, Virginia, USA

❏ Jack Rabbit — Clementon Lake Park, New Jersey, USA

❏ Jack Rabbit — Kennywood, Pennsylvania, USA

❏ Jack Rabbit — Sea Breeze, New York, USA

❏ Judge Roy Scream — Six Flags Over Texas, Texas, USA

❏ Kiddie Coaster — Playland, New York, USA

❏ Leap the Dips — Lakemont Park, Pennsylvania, USA

❏ Le Monstre — La Ronde, Quebec, Canada

❏ Lil' Dipper — Camden Park, West Virginia, USA

❏ Little Dipper — Hillcrest Park, Illinois, USA

❏ Little Dipper — Melrose Park, Illinois, USA

❏ Mean Streak — Cedar Point, Ohio, USA

❏ Mighty Canadian Minebuster — Paramount Canada's Wonderland, Ontario, Canada

❏ Outlaw — Adventureland, Iowa, USA

❏ Pegasus — Big Chief, Wisconsin, USA

❏ Phoenix — Knoebel's Amusement Resort, Pennsylvania, USA

❏ Predator — Darien Lake Theme Park, New York, USA

❏ Psyclone — Six Flags Magic Mountain, California, USA

❏ Racer — Kennywood, Pennsylvania, USA

❏ Racer — Paramount's Kings Island, Ohio, USA

❏ Raging Wolf Bobs — Geauga Lake, Ohio, USA

❏ Rattler — Six Flags Fiesta Texas, Texas, USA

❏ Raven — Holiday World, Indiana, USA

❏ Rebel Yell — Paramount's Kings Dominion, Virginia, USA

❑ Riverside Cyclone   Riverside Park, Massachusetts, USA
❑ Roller Coaster   Joyland, Kansas, USA
❑ Roller Coaster   Lagoon, Utah, USA
❑ Roller Coaster   Playland, British Columbia, Canada
❑ Roller Coaster   Western Washington Fairgrounds,
                            Washington, USA
❑ Rolling Thunder   Six Flags Great Adventure, New Jersey, USA
❑ Rollo Coaster   Idlewild Park, Pennsylvania, USA
❑ Sea Dragon   Wyandot Lake, Ohio, USA
❑ Scooby Doo   Paramount's Kings Dominion, Virginia, USA
❑ Scooby Doo's   Paramount's Carowinds, North Carolina, USA
     Ghoster Coaster
❑ Screamin' Eagle   Six Flags St. Louis, Missouri, USA
❑ Screechin' Eagle   Americana, Ohio, USA
❑ Serpiente de Fuego   La Fería, Mexico
❑ Skyliner   Lakemont Park, Pennsylvania, USA
❑ Sky Princess   Dutch Wonderland, Pennsylvania, USA
❑ Starliner   Miracle Strip, Florida, USA
❑ Swamp Fox   Family Kingdom, South Carolina, USA
❑ Texas Cyclone   Six Flags Astroworld, Texas, USA
❑ Texas Giant   Six Flags Over Texas, Texas, USA
❑ Thunderbolt   Kennywood, Pennsylvania, USA
❑ Thunderbolt   Riverside Park, Massachusetts, USA
❑ Thunder Hawk   Dorney Park, Pennsylvania, USA
❑ Thunder Road   Paramount's Carowinds, North Carolina, USA
❑ Thunder Run   Kentucky Kingdom, Kentucky, USA
❑ Timber Wolf   Worlds of Fun, Missouri, USA
❑ Tornado   Adventureland, Iowa, USA
❑ Tornado   Stricker's Grove, Ohio, USA
❑ Tree Topper   Upper Clements Theme Park,
                            Nova Scotia, Canada
❑ Twister II   Elitch Gardens, Colorado, USA
❑ Underground   Adventureland, Iowa, USA
❑ Viper   Six Flags Great America, Illinois, USA
❑ Wildcat   Lake Compounce, Connecticut, USA
❑ Wildcat   Hersheypark, Pennsylvania, USA
❑ Wildcat   Frontier City, Oklahoma, USA
❑ Wilde Beast   Paramount Canada's Wonderland,
                            Ontario, Canada
❑ Wild One   Adventure World, Maryland, USA
❑ Wolverine Wildcat   Michigan's Adventure, Michigan, USA

❑ Yankee Cannonball   Canobie Lake Park, New Hampshire, USA
❑ Zach's Zoomer   Michigan's Adventure, Michigan, USA
❑ Zeus   Big Chief, Wisconsin, USA
❑ Zingo   Bell's Amusement Park, Oklahoma, USA
❑ Zippin' Pippin   Libertyland, Tennessee, USA

Roller Coaster Fact: The Wild One, currently operating at Adventure World in Maryland, originally began its life in 1917 at Paragon Park, outside of Boston, Massachusetts, where it was called the Giant Coaster and was a favorite of the Kennedy clan.

11 THE WORLD'S MAJOR STEEL COASTERS

(Listed alphabetically, by continent. Listing includes the name of the ride, the park, and the country. Check off in the box provided each roller coaster that you have ridden.)

ASIA

❑ Andalusian Railroad	Portopia Land, Japan
❑ Bandit	Yomiuriland, Japan
❑ Bavarian Mountain Railroad	Portopia Land, Japan
❑ Big Thunder Mountain Railroad	Tokyo Disneyland, Japan
❑ Corkscrew	Nagashima Spaland, Japan
❑ DIOS	Mukogaoka, Japan
❑ Double Loop	Portopia Land, Japan
❑ Dragon	Ocean Park, China
❑ Fortress of Eagle	Everland, Korea
❑ F:2	Nasu Highlands, Japan
❑ Fujiyama	Fujikyu Highlands, Japan
❑ Hayabusa	Summerland, Japan
❑ Loop Corkscrew	Expoland, Japan
❑ Looping Star	Nagashima Spaland, Japan
❑ Loop Screw	Seibu-en, Japan
❑ Moonsault Scramble	Fujikyu Highlands, Japan
❑ Roller Coaster	Koraku-en, Japan
❑ Stand-up Coaster	Family Land, Japan
❑ Super Roller Coaster	Fantasy Dome, Japan

❏ Surf Coaster	Hakkeijima Sea Paradise, Japan
❏ Titan	Space World, Japan
❏ Orochi	Expoland, Japan

AUSTRALIA

❏ Lethal Weapon—The Ride	Warner Bros. Movie World, Australia
❏ Thunderbolt	Dreamworld, Australia
❏ Tower of Terror	Dreamworld, Australia
❏ Vampire	Australia's Wonderland, Australia

EUROPE

❏ Air Race	Bobbejaanland, Belgium
❏ Avalanche	Blackpool Pleasure Beach, England
❏ Big Loop	Heide Park, Germany
❏ Big Thunder Mountain Railroad	Disneyland Paris, France
❏ Black Hole	Alton Towers, England
❏ Bobbahn 1	Heide Park, Germany
❏ Bobbahn 2	Heide Park, Germany
❏ Bullet	Flamingo Land, England
❏ Colorado	Walibi, Belgium
❏ Colorado Adventure	Phantasialand, Germany
❏ Corkscrew	Alton Towers, England
❏ Corkscrew	Flamingo Land, England
❏ Dragon Khan	Port Aventura, Spain
❏ El Condor	Walibi Flavo, The Netherlands
❏ El Diablo	Port Aventura, Spain
❏ Euro Mir	Europa Park, Germany
❏ Gebirgsbahn	Phantasialand, Germany
❏ Goudurix	Parc Astérix, France
❏ Grotten Blitz	Europa Park, Germany
❏ Hangover	Liseberg, Sweden
❏ Hochbahn	Prater Park, Austria
❏ Jetline	Grona Lund, Sweden
❏ Le Temple de Péril	Disneyland Paris, France
❏ Lethal Weapon—The Ride	Warner Bros. Movie World, Germany
❏ Lisebergbanen	Liseberg, Sweden
❏ Looping Bahn	Prater Park, Austria
❏ Looping Star	Bobbejaanland, Belgium

❏ Looping Star   Great Yarmouth Pleasure Beach, England

❏ Nemesis   Alton Towers, England

❏ Nessie   Hansa Park, Germany

❏ Pepsi Max Big One   Blackpool Pleasure Beach, England

❏ Python   De Eftelling, The Netherlands

❏ Rat   Lightwater Valley, England

❏ Revolution   Blackpool Pleasure Beach, England

❏ Revolution   Bobbejaanland, Belgium

❏ 7-Up Shockwave   Drayton Manor, England

❏ Sirocco   Walibi, Belgium

❏ Space Center   Phantasialand, Germany

❏ Space Comet   Walibi Stroumpf, France

❏ Space Invaders   Blackpool Pleasure Beach, England

❏ Space Mountain   Disneyland Paris, France

❏ Steeplechase   Blackpool Pleasure Beach, England

❏ Thunder Looper   Alton Towers, England

❏ Thunder Mountain   Flamingo Land, England

❏ Tornado   Bobbejaanland, Belgium

❏ Tower of Terror   Camelot, England

❏ Ultimate   Lightwater Valley, England

❏ Vampire   Chessington World of Adventures, England

❏ X:/No Way Out   Thorpe Park, England

NORTH AMERICA

(These listings also include the state or province, where applicable.)

❏ Adventure Express   Paramount's Kings Island, Ohio, USA

❏ Alpengeist   Busch Gardens, Virginia, USA

❏ Anaconda   Paramount's Kings Dominion, Virginia, USA

❏ Auto Sled   Galaxyland, Alberta, Canada

❏ Avalanche   Paramount's Kings Dominion, Virginia, USA

❏ Bat   Paramount Canada's Wonderland, Ontario, Canada

❏ Batman and Robin—The Chiller   Six Flags Great Adventure, New Jersey, USA

~~~~~~

Roller Coaster Fact: There are currently over one dozen roller coasters themed to motion picture properties. Not surprisingly, all are located in theme parks owned by companies that also own movie studios.

~~~~~~

❏ Batman—The Escape   Six Flags Astroworld, Texas, USA
❏ Batman—The Ride   Six Flags Great Adventure,
                                      New Jersey, USA
❏ Batman—The Ride   Six Flags Great America,
                                      Illinois, USA
❏ Batman—The Ride   Six Flags Magic Mountain,
                                      California, USA
❏ Batman—The Ride   Six Flags Over Georgia,
                                      Georgia, USA
❏ Batman—The Ride   Six Flags St. Louis, Missouri, USA
❏ Big Bad Wolf   Busch Gardens, Virginia, USA
❏ Big Thunder Mountain Railroad Disneyland, California, USA
❏ Big Thunder Mountain Railroad Magic Kingdom at Walt Disney
                                      World, Florida, USA
❏ Blazing Fury   Dollywood, Tennessee, USA
❏ Bobsleds   Sea Breeze, New York, USA
❏ Boomerang   Knott's Berry Farm, California, USA
❏ Boomerang—Coast to Coaster   The Great Escape, New York, USA
❏ Canyon Blaster   Grand Slam Canyon, Nevada, USA
❏ Carolina Cyclone   Paramount's Carowinds,
                                      North Carolina, USA
❏ Carolina Gold Rusher   Paramount's Carowinds,
                                      North Carolina, USA
❏ Cedar Creek Mine Ride   Cedar Point, Ohio, USA
❏ Chang   Kentucky Kingdom, USA
❏ Chaos   Opryland, Tennessee, USA
❏ Cobra   La Ronde, Quebec, Canada
❏ Colossal Fire Dragon   Lagoon, Utah, USA
❏ Corkscrew   Cedar Point, Ohio, USA
❏ Corkscrew   Playland, British Columbia, Canada
❏ Corkscrew   Valleyfair!, Minnesota, USA
❏ Dahlonega Mine Train   Six Flags Over Georgia, Georgia, USA
❏ Demon   Paramount's Great America,
                                      California, USA

❑ Demon   Six Flags Great America,
                                          Illinois, USA

❑ Desert Storm   Castles and Coasters, Arizona, USA
❑ Desperado   Buffalo Bill's, Nevada, USA
❑ Disaster Transport   Cedar Point, Ohio, USA
❑ Double Loop   Geauga Lake, Ohio, USA
❑ Drachen Fire   Busch Gardens, Virginia, USA
❑ Dragon   Adventureland, Iowa, USA
❑ Dragon Fyre   Paramount Canada's Wonderland,
                                          Ontario, Canada

❑ Dragon Mountain   Marineland, Ontario, Canada
❑ Excalibur   Six Flags Astroworld, Texas, USA
❑ Excalibur   Valleyfair!, Minnesota, USA
❑ Flashback   Six Flags Magic Mountain,
                                          California, USA

❑ Flashback   Six Flags Over Texas, Texas, USA
❑ Gemini   Cedar Point, Ohio, USA
❑ Golden Nugget Mine Ride   Dinosaur Beach, New Jersey, USA
❑ Gold Rusher   Six Flags Magic Mountain,
                                          California, USA

❑ Gravity Defying Corkscrew   Silverwood, Idaho, USA
❑ Great American Scream Machine   Six Flags Great Adventure,
                                          New Jersey, USA

❑ Great Nor'Easter   Morey's Pier, New Jersey, USA
❑ Great White   Sea World of Texas, Texas, USA
❑ Greezed Lightnin'   Six Flags Astroworld, Texas, USA
❑ Hangman   Opryland, Tennessee, USA
❑ High Roller   Stratosphere Tower, Nevada, USA
❑ Hurricane   Adventureland, New York, USA
❑ Hurricane   Playland, New York, USA
❑ Iron Dragon   Cedar Point, Ohio, USA
❑ Iron Wolf   Six Flags Great America,
                                          Illinois, USA

❑ Jaguar   Knott's Berry Farm, California, USA
❑ Joker's Revenge   Six Flags Fiesta Texas, Texas, USA
❑ King Cobra   Paramount's Kings Island,
                                          Ohio, USA

❑ Kumba   Busch Gardens, Florida, USA
❑ Laser   Dorney Park, Pennsylvania, USA
❑ La Vibora   Six Flags Over Texas, Texas, USA
❑ Le Boomerang   La Ronde, Quebec, Canada

❏ Le Dragon	La Ronde, Quebec, Canada
❏ Le Super Ménage	La Ronde, Quebec, Canada
❏ Loch Ness Monster	Busch Gardens, Virginia, USA
❏ Magnum XL-200	Cedar Point, Ohio, USA
❏ Manhattan Express	New York New York, Nevada, USA
❏ Mantis	Cedar Point, Ohio, USA
❏ Matterhorn	Disneyland, California, USA
❏ Mayan Mindbender	Six Flags Astroworld, Texas, USA
❏ Mr. Freeze	Six Flags Over Texas, Texas, USA
❏ Mr. Freeze	Six Flags St. Louis, Missouri, USA
❏ Mindbender	Galaxyland, Alberta, Canada
❏ Mind Bender	Six Flags Over Georgia, Georgia, USA
❏ Mind Eraser	Adventure World, Maryland, USA
❏ Mind Eraser	Darien Lake Theme Park, New York, USA
❏ Mind Eraser	Elitch Gardens, Colorado, USA
❏ Mind Eraser	Geauga Lake, Ohio, USA
❏ Mind Eraser	Riverside Park, Massachusetts, USA
❏ Montezooma's Revenge	Knott's Berry Farm, California, USA
❏ Montu	Busch Gardens, Florida, USA
❏ Ninja	Six Flags Magic Mountain, California, USA
❏ Ninja	Six Flags Over Georgia, Georgia, USA
❏ Ninja	Six Flags St. Louis, Missouri, USA
❏ Orient Express	Worlds of Fun, Missouri, USA
❏ Outer Limits Flight of Fear	Paramount's Kings Dominion, Virginia, USA
❏ Outer Limits Flight of Fear	Paramount's Kings Island, Ohio, USA
❏ Polar Coaster	Story Land, New Hampshire, USA
❏ Python	Busch Gardens, Florida, USA
❏ Quantum Loop	Sea Breeze, New York, USA
❏ Raptor	Cedar Point, Ohio, USA
❏ Red Devil	Ghost Town in the Sky, North Carolina, USA
❏ Revolution	Six Flags Magic Mountain, California, USA
❏ Revolution	Libertyland, Tennessee, USA
❏ Ripsaw	Knott's Camp Snoopy, Minnesota, USA

❑ River King Mine Ride   Six Flags St. Louis, Missouri, USA
❑ Road Runner Express   Six Flags Fiesta Texas, Texas, USA
❑ Rock 'n' Roller Coaster   Opryland, Tennessee, USA
❑ Runaway Mine Train   Six Flags Over Texas, Texas, USA
❑ Runaway Mountain   Six Flags Over Texas, Texas, USA
❑ Runaway Train   Six Flags Great Adventure, New Jersey, USA

❑ Santa's Rapid Transit   Santa's Village, New Hampshire, USA

❑ Scandia Screamer   Scandia Family Fun Center, California, USA

❑ Scorpion   Busch Gardens, Florida, USA
❑ Screamin' Delta Demon   Opryland, Tennessee, USA
❑ Sea Serpent   Mariner's Landing, New Jersey, USA
❑ Shockwave   Paramount's Kings Dominion, Virginia, USA

❑ Shockwave   Six Flags Great America, Illinois, USA

❑ Shockwave   Six Flags Over Texas, Texas, USA
❑ Sidewinder   Hersheypark, Pennsylvania, USA
❑ Silver Bullet   Frontier City, Oklahoma, USA
❑ Skull Mountain   Six Flags Great Adventure, New Jersey, USA

❑ Skyrider   Paramount Canada's Wonderland, Ontario, Canada

❑ sooperdooperLooper   Hersheypark, Pennsylvania, USA
❑ Space Mountain   Disneyland, California, USA

Roller Coaster Fact: The Space Mountain coasters located in Disneyland, Walt Disney World's Magic Kingdom, and Disneyland Paris are hardly identical installations. The California version is a single-tracked, swooping, spiraling thriller, with short trains seating passengers side by side. The Florida ride is a dual-tracked model with two cars linked together to provide six-passenger tandem seating, and it appears to be based on the design of Disneyland's Matterhorn. The Paris coaster features long, traditional-style coaster trains and goes upside down several times. All three share the same space-traveling theme, however.

❏ Space Mountain	Magic Kingdom at Walt Disney World, Florida, USA
❏ Steamin' Demon	The Great Escape, New York, USA
❏ Steel Force	Dorney Park, Pennsylvania, USA
❏ Steel Phantom	Kennywood, Pennsylvania, USA
❏ Superman—The Escape	Six Flags Magic Mountain, California, USA
❏ Texas Tornado	Wonderland, Texas, USA
❏ Thunderation	Silver Dollar City, Missouri, USA
❏ Thunderbolt	MGM Grand Adventures, Nevada, USA
❏ Thunder Express	Dollywood, Tennessee, USA
❏ Tidal Wave	Paramount's Great America, California, USA
❏ Tidal Wave	Trimper's Rides, Maryland, USA
❏ Top Gun	Paramount Canada's Wonderland, Ontario, Canada
❏ Top Gun	Paramount's Great America, California, USA
❏ Top Gun	Paramount's Kings Island, Ohio, USA
❏ Trailblazer	Hersheypark, Pennsylvania, USA
❏ T2	Kentucky Kingdom, Kentucky, USA
❏ Turn of the Century	Calaway Park, Alberta, Canada
❏ Ultra Twister	Six Flags Astroworld, Texas, USA
❏ Vampire	Kentucky Kingdom, Kentucky, USA
❏ Viper	Darien Lake Theme Park, New York, USA
❏ Viper	Six Flags Astroworld, Texas, USA
❏ Viper	Six Flags Great Adventure, New Jersey, USA
❏ Viper	Six Flags Magic Mountain, California, USA
❏ Vortex	Paramount Canada's Wonderland, Ontario, Canada
❏ Vortex	Paramount's Carowinds, North Carolina, USA
❏ Vortex	Paramount's Great America, California, USA
❏ Vortex	Paramount's Kings Island, Ohio, USA

❑ Wabash Cannonball   Opryland, Tennessee, USA
❑ West Coaster   Pacific Pier, California, USA
❑ Whirlwind   Knoebel's, Pennsylvania, USA
❑ Whizzer   Six Flags Great America,
                               Illinois, USA
❑ Wilde Maus   Busch Gardens, Virginia, USA
❑ Wild Mouse   Idlewild Park, Pennsylvania, USA
❑ Wild Thing   Valleyfair!, Minnesota, USA
❑ Windjammer   Knott's Berry Farm, California, USA
❑ XLR-8   Six Flags Astroworld, Texas, USA
❑ Zambezi Zinger   Worlds of Fun, Missouri, USA
❑ Zoomerang   Lake Compounce, Connecticut, USA

12 FUN TOP FIVE ROLLER COASTER LISTS

Now that you're really a diehard fan of roller coasters, simple top ten lists just won't do anymore. True lovers of roller coasters go beyond listing the best wood or steel rides, compiling data in even the most obscure coaster categories—like these:

FIVE BEST INVERTED COASTERS

1. ALPENGEIST, Busch Gardens, Williamsburg, Virginia
   Built over and through a ravine, with some amazing visuals for both riders and spectators. The sheer power of this ride and size of its elements are truly amazing.

2. MONTU, Busch Gardens, Tampa, Florida
   It's the natural evolution of the inverted roller coaster—all the best of every ride of this type is rolled into this one.

3. RAPTOR, Cedar Point, Sandusky, Ohio
   A big ride with some amazing nuances, all dictated by having to squeeze into tight spaces and build around existing structures.

4. BATMAN—THE RIDE
   Six Flags Great America, Gurnee, Illinois
   Six Flags Great Adventure, Jackson, New Jersey
   Six Flags Magic Mountain, Valencia, California
   Six Flags St. Louis, Allenton, Missouri
   Six Flags Over Georgia, Atlanta, Georgia

Alpengeist, Busch Gardens, Williamsburg. (Courtesy of Busch Gardens)

~~~~~~

Roller Coaster Fact: Only one roller coaster at a time can hold the title of the best coaster in the world, but since the 1960s (when this type of rating first became prominent), many have held the position. Among the coasters to hold top title are the Cyclone, Coney Island; Thunderbolt, Kennywood; Beast, Paramount's Kings Island; Texas Cyclone, Six Flags Astroworld; Riverside Cyclone, Riverside Park; Timber Wolf, Worlds of Fun; Magnum XL-200, Cedar Point; and Texas Giant, Six Flags Over Texas.

~~~~~~

Identical thrill machines, with the Missouri version a mirror image of the other four. Compact and relentless.

5.   THE GREAT NOR'EASTER, Morey's Pier, North Wildwood, New Jersey
One of nearly a dozen identical installations worldwide, this version is distinguished by winding in, around, above, and below other existing attractions on this oceanside pier, with some truly harrowing tight squeezes and clearances.

FIVE BEST STAND-UP COASTERS

1.   MANTIS, Cedar Point, Sandusky, Ohio
A super-intense experience, with lightning-quick elements, a demented layout, and a beautiful setting, partially over a lake.

2.   CHANG, Kentucky Kingdom, Louisville, Kentucky
Almost a copy of Mantis, but slightly larger and adding one more inversion in place of Mantis's spaghetti-bowl figure-eight finale.

3.   VORTEX, Paramount's Great America, Santa Clara, California
Very enjoyable ride with a twisting double dip that literally lifts you off your feet.

4.   IRON WOLF, Six Flags Great America, Gurnee, Illinois
Wild layout, with a figure-eight finale featuring many sudden changes of direction.

5.   BATMAN—THE ESCAPE, Six Flags Astroworld, Houston, Texas
Heavily themed attraction, with a queue line that is almost as much fun as the ride itself.

Opposite Page: Cedar Point's Mantis, an example of a stand-up coaster. (Courtesy of Dan Feicht, Cedar Point)

~~~~~~

Roller Coaster Fact: The five tallest looping roller coasters in the world: Manhattan Express (203 feet), New York New York Resort and Casino, Las Vegas, Nevada; Alpengeist (195 feet), Busch Gardens, Williamsburg, Virginia; Viper (188 feet), Six Flags Magic Mountain, Valencia, California; Great American Scream Machine (173 feet), Six Flags Great Adventure, Jackson, New Jersey; Shock Wave (170 feet), Six Flags Great America, Gurnee, Illinois.

~~~~~~

FIVE BEST MINE TRAINS

1. BIG THUNDER MOUNTAIN RAILROAD, The Magic Kingdom at Walt Disney World, Orlando, Florida
The perfect example of what this type of ride should be, heavily themed throughout in true Disney fashion.

2. ADVENTURE EXPRESS, Paramount's Kings Island, Cincinnati, Ohio
Special-effects-laden terrain ride with unexpected drops and hidden turns.

3. RUNAWAY TRAIN, Six Flags Over Texas, Arlington, Texas
The world's first-ever mine train roller coaster still has what it takes. Hidden tunnels and truly inspired twisting, dropping trackage.

4. THUNDERATION, Silver Dollar City, Branson, Missouri
The world's fastest mine-train-type attraction. Using the park's natural terrain, the ride gets going right out of the station and doesn't have a lift-hill until the very end, which leads into a perilous final drop, the longest on a mine train. Several seats on the ride face backward.

5. THUNDER EXPRESS, Dollywood, Pigeon Forge, Tennessee
Perfect for this park, a family ride featuring many of the thrills of bigger, more action-packed coasters.

FIVE BEST ENCLOSED COASTERS

1. SPACE MOUNTAIN, Disneyland, Anaheim, California
Very different from the Florida version. This one has similar theming, but its layout is more dynamic, with better turns and drops.

Children of all ages thrill to the charms of Walt Disney World's Big Thunder Mountain Railroad, rated best mine train. (Courtesy of Walt Disney World)

~~~~~~

Roller Coaster Fact: The Cyclone Racer at the Pike in Long Beach, California (dismantled in 1968), was the first roller coaster movie star. It made appearances in *The Beast From 20,000 Fathoms, Strike Me Pink,* Abbott and Costello's *The Dancing Masters,* and *It's A Mad, Mad, Mad, Mad World,* among others.

~~~~~~

2.   OUTER LIMITS FLIGHT OF FEAR
     Paramount's Kings Dominion, Doswell, Virginia
     Paramount's Kings Island, Cincinnati, Ohio

Identical attractions with amazing theming and tight twisting layouts. These rides feature four inversions. Of more special note, they are the first full-circuit roller coasters to use a linear induction launch system. Instead of rolling casually out of the station onto a lift-hill, the trains catapult from 0 to 60 mph into an interior lit by strobes and multicolored spotlights.

3.   SPACE MOUNTAIN, Disneyland Paris, Paris, France
     Its theming is similar to Disney's Space Mountains, but this one has a long, more traditional coaster train rocketing up a lift-hill into a real upside-down roller coaster.

4.   SPACE MOUNTAIN, The Magic Kingdom at Walt Disney World, Orlando, Florida
     The original, and predecessor to its Disneyland cousin. A dual-tracked ride (one side is a mirror image of the other) with toboggan-style seating. Although Disney has never made the comparison, this ride is extremely similar in setup and layout to the world's original steel coaster, Disneyland's Matterhorn.

5.   DISASTER TRANSPORT, Cedar Point, Sandusky, Ohio
     A bobsled-type ride themed to a space journey, final destination Alaska. Pay attention to the detail in the theming and story line here—someone with a great sense of humor put this all together.

FIVE BEST WOODEN TERRAIN COASTERS

1.   BEAST, Paramount's Kings Island, Cincinnati, Ohio
     The granddaddy of all terrain coasters, this is also the longest wooden roller coaster in the world. Two lift-hills lead into a fast trip over thirty-five

The Beast, Paramount's Kings Island. (Courtesy of Paramount's Kings Island)

acres of wooded, rolling land in the back of the park. You can't see much of this ride from any vantage point in or out of the park; therefore, its many pleasures remain a mystery to first-time riders.

2. RAVEN, Holiday World, Santa Claus, Indiana
   Sudden drops and tight turns are the standout features of this sort of mini-Beast. It doesn't have the sheer power of the larger ride, nor is it as psychologically challenging, and it is significantly shorter in both track length and ride time, but in many ways it is a better "traditional" roller coaster.

3. THUNDERBOLT, Kennywood, West Mifflin, Pennsylvania
   Built over a ravine, it features significant drops right out of the station, a lift-hill mid-course, and what really sets it apart from any other coaster in the world: two near-100-foot drops at the very end, just before the return to the loading dock.

4. HERCULES, Dorney Park, Allentown, Pennsylvania
   This beauty resides on a hillside and features the second-longest wooden coaster drop in the entire world. The drop leads into a high-banked flat speed turn at the bottom before returning to the top of the hill. The rest of the ride can't even approach that intensity, and therefore doesn't try.

~~~~~~

Roller Coaster Fact: The five longest wooden roller coaster drops in the world: Hercules (157 feet), Dorney Park, Allentown, Pennsylvania; Mean Streak (155 feet), Cedar Point, Sandusky, Ohio; American Eagle (147 feet), Six Flags Great America, Gurnee, Illinois; Beast (141 feet), Paramount's Kings Island, Cincinnati, Ohio; Texas Giant (137 feet), Six Flags Over Texas, Arlington, Texas.

~~~~~~

5. JACK RABBIT, Sea Breeze, Rochester, New York
A dwarf among giants, but try riding this classic 1921 ride at night for the first time. While the first drop is the largest by far, some of the final drops are significantly deeper than ones much earlier in the ride, and there's a real hoot of a surprise at the end.

FIVE BEST SUSPENDED COASTERS

1. TOP GUN, Paramount's Kings Island, Cincinnati, Ohio
A brief but extremely intense experience. Spanning a ravine, the swinging cars fly through the course with abandonment, and you'll be convinced that collision with a support post is imminent. Doesn't even come close to giving you a moment to catch your breath.

2. NINJA, Six Flags Magic Mountain, Valencia, California
This ride's highest point is on top of the mini-mountain in the center of this park. From there, it's non-stop as the layout winds down one side of the mountain—above walkways and entangled with other rides—with the cars swinging at times to 10 degrees above horizontal.

3. BIG BAD WOLF, Busch Gardens, Williamsburg, Virginia
The world's first successful suspended roller coaster. Heavily themed throughout the course, with trains traveling through a village, which leads to the grand finale—a large drop into an S-turn over water. One of the best-loved roller coasters in the world.

4. FORTRESS OF EAGLE, Everland, Korea
The tallest suspended roller coaster in the world, this ride also utilizes natural terrain to provide a stunning array of large drops and high-speed twisting turns.

Top Gun, Paramount's Kings Island. (Courtesy of Paramount's Kings Island)

5. VORTEX, Paramount Canada's Wonderland, Vaughan, Ontario, Canada
    A twin of the aforementioned Top Gun (this one came first). Vortex begins on a man-made mountain and ends over a lake.

FIVE BEST MEGA-COASTERS

1. STEEL FORCE, Dorney Park, Allentown, Pennsylvania
    Similar to Magnum in layout and pacing, this one features a first drop into an underground tunnel, an amazing helix, and a stunning finale of air-time-filled rabbit hops.

2. MAGNUM XL-200, Cedar Point, Sandusky, Ohio
    The first full-circuit roller coaster ever to stretch over 200 feet high, this masterpiece still hasn't been topped in its ability to provide spills, chills, and thrills. Magnum features no inversions—it relies instead on a well-paced series of large drops and totally wild smaller hills.

3. FUJIYAMA, Fujikyu Highlands, Osaka, Japan
    Godzilla is no longer the largest monster ever to conquer Japan. At 259 feet, this is the world's tallest full-circuit roller coaster. Unlike other 200-foot-

plus coasters, which are designed as out and backs, this one is a twister, loosely based on the Coney Island Cyclone.

4.   BANDIT, Yomiuriland, Tokyo, Japan
This was the world's first huge non-looping steel roller coaster. Not only does it feature a large lift-hill and first drop, but it also dives into a ravine, providing it with a vertical spread of over 250 feet.

5.   PEPSI MAX BIG ONE, Blackpool Pleasure Beach, Blackpool, England
Towering over the Irish Sea, this ride has track and structure winding over, under, and through at least four of the park's other roller coasters.

FIVE BEST AIRTIME COASTERS

1.   COMET, The Great Escape, Lake George, New York
It is impossible to remain totally seated during this ride. There are more moments that lift you out of your seat than any other ride in the world. In fact, there are more moments of negative gravity on this ride than the ride itself has hills to provide them.

2.   HURLER
Paramount's Carowinds, Charlotte, North Carolina
Paramount's Kings Dominion, Doswell, Virginia

A rare pair of identical wooden roller coasters, each with large first drops leading into a series of low hills, each providing amazingly orchestrated floating negative g's.

3.   BIG DIPPER, Geauga Lake, Aurora, Ohio
This 1920s classic is the way roller coasters used to be. It doesn't have great height—although it *was* the world's *longest* roller coaster when it was built. Each hill either lifts or throws you out of your seat, and several bends in the track seize the moment you're flying and throw you to the side as well.

4.   THUNDER RUN, Kentucky Kingdom, Louisville, Kentucky
This is the original design that the Paramount Hurlers were based on. It has the same moments of negative gravity as the previously mentioned pair, but on this ride, passengers don't "float" out of the seat—they get *launched* out.

5.   BLUE STREAK, Cedar Point, Sandusky, Ohio
Perfectly designed to provide maximum airtime, this one has choppy little hops and humps, all taken at top speed.

FIVE BEST FIRST DROPS

1. RIVERSIDE CYCLONE, Riverside Park, Agawam, Massachusetts

The trackage that comprises the first few hundred feet after the lift-hill on this ride is without doubt the finest, most intense wooden roller coaster design in existence. This is not just your ordinary over-the-lift, plunge-to-the-ground drop. At the top, there's a large-radius vertical curve, which sets up a ledge that the train drops off of sharply, at a 54-degree angle. On the way down, the track begins to bank to the right; two-thirds of the way down, the train severely slams into a 60-degree banked turn, where it begins to rise. As it completes the turn, it reaches to almost half the height of the initial plunge before it dives down again, this time all the way to the ground, all the while banked on its side. This section of track has been described as the most severe wooden roller coaster moment ever built. There won't be any arguments against that fact here. (And the rest of the ride's pretty amazing, too!)

2. RAPTOR, Cedar Point, Sandusky, Ohio

It's an elongated S-curve, with a sudden drop-off near the top that may provide the best free-falling sensation of any coaster currently operating.

3. CYCLONE, Astroland (at Coney Island), Brooklyn, New York

One of the steepest roller coaster drops in the world, this one has a slight twist to the right at the top, during which the train descends slightly. Then it sharply plunges to the ground at a 57-degree angle.

The Riverside Cyclone's first drop is probably the most thrilling section of any roller coaster in the world. (Author's Collection)

~~~~~~

Roller Coaster Fact: Charles Lindbergh is quoted as saying that a ride on the Coney Island Cyclone was more exciting than a transatlantic flight.

~~~~~~

4.   FUJIYAMA, Fujikyu Highlands, Osaka, Japan
Does pretty much what the Coney Island Cyclone does, except does it on steel, at a steeper angle, and at almost three times the height.

5.   GREAT WHITE, Wild Wheels Pier, Wildwood, New Jersey
It's high (120 feet), it's steep (over 57 degrees), and its first drop happens immediately off the sharp lift-hill crest. *And* it dives into a structure resembling the eye of a storm, which is built directly over the sand of this Atlantic Coast beach. Just before you plummet, look straight out—that's a brief unobstructed view of the Atlantic Ocean you'll be getting.

FIVE BEST FINISHES

1.   BEAST, Paramount's Kings Island, Cincinnati, Ohio
While most of this ride is set low to the ground on rolling terrain, a second lift-hill sets up its finish. At the top, the train rolls into a 141-foot-long drop (the longest on the entire ride). This drop, set at a shallow 18-degree angle, builds up the highest speed during the ride and leads into a huge, upward 540-degree partially tunneled helix.

2.   TEXAS GIANT, Six Flags Over Texas, Arlington, Texas
Over the first two-thirds of this ride, you get large, twisting drops and sudden changes of direction. Nearing the finish, the trains suddenly pick up speed on track that dives into the dense wooden structure of the ride, enveloping riders within walls of timber, as the track wraps around the entire main structure on a series of small hops taken at breathless speeds.

3.   RAVEN, Holiday World, Santa Claus, Indiana
More than halfway through the course, a large drop plunges passengers into a valley. The track veers to avoid a large tree, and the coaster roars to a finish on a large banked turn, twisting to the left into the station.

4.   THUNDERBOLT, Kennywood, West Mifflin, Pennsylvania
Situated on the edge of a ravine, the first drop on this ride is a 40-footer, right out of the station. The final two drops are the largest on the ride, at 80 and 90 feet, respectively, and come after a series of rambunctious right-hand turns and drops.

5.   BIG BAD WOLF, Busch Gardens, Williamsburg, Virginia

The first half of the ride is swift and playful. A second lift-hill carries passengers to the highest point, before dropping them down a hillside to a river, then into a wickedly twisted S-turn.

FIVE BEST TUNNELS

1.   BEAST, Paramount's Kings Island, Cincinnati, Ohio

Some roller coasters are lucky to have one tunnel, if any at all. This one has three. The best are the first one, an underground burrow that the first drop plunges into, and the last, which partially encloses the 540-degree helix that makes up the finale.

2.   GRIZZLY, Paramount's Kings Dominion, Doswell, Virginia

It's brief, but is totally hidden, and comes at a moment immediately after passengers have been launched off their seats in an exquisite moment of air-time. Look out! The tunnel looks too small to allow the train to fit into it, and it contains a surprise!

3.   WILD ONE, Adventure World, Largo, Maryland

A new water ride slashes back and forth through the structure of this coaster, and part of the theme of the new wet ride is a large mountain struc-ture, which the coaster dives toward, then under.

4.   MONTU, Busch Gardens, Tampa, Florida

While not a dark tunnel, this brief moment underground brings passen-gers' dangling feet to within inches of the ground. Upon exiting the tunnel, the train heads directly toward a wall of concrete, all the while rising up into an inversion.

5.   FLYER COMET, Whalom Park, Lunenburg, Massachusetts

This classic wooden ride has been around since the 1940s. The tunnel, dubbed the "Black Hole," was added in the 1990s. It's an extremely dark exer-cise in terror, surprisingly long, and features several surprises.

FIVE BEST NIGHT RIDES

1.   BEAST, Paramount's Kings Island, Cincinnati, Ohio

This ride just keeps popping up on our lists, doesn't it? At one time, the mile and a half of track was completely unlit by electric lights. Lately, more and more lights have appeared, making the Beast almost as brightly lit at night as it is in the daytime. It's not a bright white light, though, but rather orange-hued, which still allows a certain amount of mystery to exist. Simply wear a secured pair of dark glasses, and the darkness returns in full force. It's worth playing this game, because the increased speed this ride has during the evening hours is incredible, and the sense of being swallowed by the woods just simply cannot be beat.

2.   RAVEN, Holiday World, Santa Claus, Indiana
While the Beast is totally removed from the rest of the park it resides in, much of the Raven is too close to the park's brightly lit attractions and parking lots, but the ride's finale takes place in dark woods and is pitch black.

3.   MAGNUM XL-200, Cedar Point, Sandusky, Ohio
Only the lift-hill has lights of any kind on it. The rest of the structure, removed from the park proper, is dark, and its Lake Erie shoreline location provides a huge, dark void. You'll feel like you've been swallowed into a black hole.

4.   GREAT WHITE, Wild Wheels Pier, Wildwood, New Jersey
The entire structure is magnificently floodlit, casting eerie shadows on the night sky. Beyond that, the Atlantic Ocean provides the same benefit that Lake Erie does for the abovementioned Magnum XL-200.

5.   MEAN STREAK, Cedar Point, Sandusky, Ohio
The world's largest wooden roller coaster, this natural, unpainted wooden structure is floodlit by three different shades of yellow light. A giant, shimmering golden jewel, with lights and shadows playing in the sky, and Lake Erie serving as a black velvet void, plus several hills that are not lit at their bases, providing a few bottomless pits.

FIVE MOST BEAUTIFUL ROLLER COASTERS

(All wood coasters, incidentally)

1.   MEAN STREAK, Cedar Point, Sandusky, Ohio
By night, this isn't just a roller coaster. It's a pile of gold, sculpted to resemble a roller coaster. By day, just as impressive; the dense structure is overpowering and is designed with true symmetry. The queue line is totally within the structure. Passengers waiting to ride will feel insignificant as they stand surrounded by these huge walls of wooden latticework.

2.   SCREAMIN' EAGLE, Six Flags St. Louis, Allenton, Missouri
The park sits on a hillside, traveling about halfway up the slope. At the park's highest point sits this gorgeous white wooden structure, a classic out-

Mean Streak, Cedar Point. (Courtesy of Dan Feicht, Cedar Point)

and-back design that runs the entire length of the park. Truly a masterpiece of roller coaster design as art.

3. GREAT AMERICAN SCREAM MACHINE, Six Flags Over Georgia, Atlanta, Georgia
    Another breathtaking example of coaster sculpture. Beautiful lines, fluid curves, and partially reflected in a lake.

4. GIANT DIPPER, Santa Cruz Beach Boardwalk, Santa Cruz, California
    Sensuously curving and dipping, this classic 1924 ride contrasts a stark, white structure with bright red track.

Roller coasters are thrilling to ride, but if they happen to be designed like Atlanta's Great American Scream Machine, they are also beautiful sculptures. (Courtesy of Bobby Nagy)

5.   WILDCAT, Hersheypark, Hershey, Pennsylvania

Gorgeous curve after curve after curve. There is not one piece of this structure that couldn't be described as graceful. Has many of the delicacies usually found only in a superbly detailed hand-made doily.

Glossary

Airtime: The sensation of lifting out of your seat when a roller coaster goes down a hill. Since you, the passenger, are lighter than the train, you become "weightless" at this moment.

Camel Back: A roller coaster hill—usually a tall one—that travels in a straight line as it goes up, over, then down.

Clothoid Loop: A 360-degree upside-down loop shaped like a teardrop.

Element: Any individual part of a roller coaster's design, such as a hill, loop, turn, etc.

Fan Turn: A horseshoe-shaped turn, usually found on wooden coasters, with its highest point at the center of the turn.

Heartline Spiral: A forward-moving, in-line inversion, which turns in a barrel-roll motion, so the rider's center of gravity shifts to the heart.

Linear Induction: A new breed of coaster-launching mechanism, using motors that create an electromagnetic current to propel the train. This allows for faster speeds and a quieter ride.

Rabbit Hop: The name given to the smaller roller coaster hills, widely known to provide the passenger with airtime.

Spaghetti Bowl: Tight, twisted coaster track, usually confined to a small area, difficult to follow and wild in nature.

Spiral Drop: The type of roller coaster drop that turns—usually a full 180 degrees—while steeply diving to the ground.

Station Air Gates: Operated using hydraulic pressure, these are the gates used to keep passengers from the track area until the time that it is safe to board the coaster train.

Transfer Track: A section of track on all coasters that mechanically moves to and from the main track, facilitating the addition or removal of trains from the circuit.

Trick-Track: A section of track with one side higher than the other, rapidly alternating, which pitches the coaster car (and passenger) from one side to the other.

Vertical Spread: A term applied to roller coasters built in ravines or other such uneven types of terrain, specifically to the height measurement from the highest point of the coaster on the highest part of the ground to the lowest point of the coaster on the lowest part of the ground.

Index

About the Author

Over the past thirty-six-plus years, *Steven J. Urbanowicz* has ridden almost 400 different coasters in more than 150 amusement parks worldwide, often trying out coasters before they are even open to the general public. He is the editor and publisher of *The Ride*, an amusement industry periodical. He lives in Jersey City, New Jersey.